Ganesh is a freelance writer and marketing professional. He has a distinct bias for the free life and loves to go off the beaten track. A great believer in human potential, he is always on the lookout for unusual stories around him.

He has written for leading publications like *Christian Science Monitor*, *Financial Chronicle*, *Spice Route*, *JetWings* and *Travel3sixty*.

You can read more about him on his website www.ganeshv.com and write to him at theholehog@yahoo.co.in or thewholehog@gmail.com.

THE UNDERAGE CEOs

*Fascinating Stories of Young Indians Who
Became CEOs in Their Twenties*

GANESH V.

COLLINS BUSINESS
An Imprint of HarperCollinsPublishers

First published in India in 2015 by Collins Business
An imprint of HarperCollins *Publishers*

Copyright © Ganesh V. 2015

P-ISBN: 978-93-5177-226-2
E-ISBN: 978-93-5177-227-9

2 4 6 8 10 9 7 5 3 1

Ganesh V. asserts the moral right
to be identified as the author of this work.

The views and opinions expressed in this book are
the author's own and the facts are as reported by him, and the
publishers are not in any way liable for the same.

All rights reserved. No part of this publication may be reproduced,
stored in a retrieval system, or transmitted, in any form or by any means,
electronic, mechanical, photocopying, recording or otherwise,
without the prior permission of the publishers.

HarperCollins *Publishers*
A-75, Sector 57, Noida, Uttar Pradesh 201301, India
1 London Bridge Street, London, SE1 9GF, United Kingdom
Hazelton Lanes, 55 Avenue Road, Suite 2900, Toronto, Ontario M5R 3L2
and 1995 Markham Road, Scarborough, Ontario M1B 5M8, Canada
25 Ryde Road, Pymble, Sydney, NSW 2073, Australia
195 Broadway, New York, NY 10007, USA

Typeset in 11.5/15 Requiem Regular at
Manipal Digital Systems, Manipal

Printed and bound at
Thomson Press (India) Ltd

For
all those who have tried to do something –
anything – original in their lives
And my family

'And those who were seen dancing were thought to be insane by those who could not hear the music.'

– Friedrich Nietzsche

Contents

Getting Started — xi

1. Web Scholarz — 1
   As an ethical hacker, Sourav Karmakar helps protect priceless online data

2. Add-on-Gyan — 25
   Priyadeep Sinha is busy igniting the minds of children with activity-based practical education

3. GharPay — 43
   Arpit Mohan and Abhishek Nayak profited early from the COD trend in e-commerce

4. iKheti — 65
   Priyanka Amar is introducing the concept of home farms to the cramped houses of Mumbai

5. Tech Innovance — 85
   Akshat Oswal and Prasad Gundecha are using artificial intelligence to automate homes

6. Biosyl Technologies — 101
   Sarah D'Souza and Amit Vernekar are making research on bacteria more cost-effective

7. iGenero — 114
Aditya Gupta and Karan Kumar are helping companies create digital strategies and forge brand identities

8. Om Shanti Traders — 134
Swati Bondia sells ethnic Indian works of art to corporates

9. Center Stage — 151
Avik Bhattacharya has channelled his passion for dance into a profitable business

10. H.H. High School — 170
S. Shadab Hassan is transforming the lives of underprivileged children in Jharkhand

11. Nurturing Green — 187
Thanks to Annu Grover, gifting plants is now a cool thing to do

12. Funding Fundas — 206

Resources — 221

Gracias — 223

Getting Started

Hi there!

Thanks for picking up this book.

You know what, you are reading it because someone asked me a question. Actually, because *several someones* asked me several questions in several college campuses.

'I have an idea. I now want to start-up. How can I do that?' Or, 'I want to be become an entrepreneur. But my parents want me to join Infosys or TCS! What should I do?' Or, 'I want to do something in the app space. Today everybody uses apps, no? So what kind can I develop?' And many other questions in the same vein.

As someone who likes mentoring college students, I listen to them carefully and do my best to guide each one of them. But when I started hearing similar questions from more and more students belonging to different colleges, I took a step back and tried to look at the trend objectively. I spoke to a number of students and professors in a few cities. I realized that, fundamentally, two things were happening:

- There is tremendous interest among college students in entrepreneurship. Many, many of them want to become entrepreneurs *right now*. Not at the age of thirty-five or forty. Many of them don't even wait till they graduate; they get started in their hostel rooms! Some of them jump in, really wanting to address a market need and do some high-quality work. Others are in it because they have heard that the life of an entrepreneur is exciting, heady – they get to be their own bosses (better still, other people report to them), do things the way they want to, come to office if and when they want to, and best of all, work in their shorts and pyjamas! If you keep at it for a few years, you will find someone to invest several million dollars in your company (or maybe, even buy you out).

- Even those who have good business ideas (ones that actually identify specific needs in the market and are aimed at solving them) are however confused about what to do next – 'How can I commercialize my idea?', 'Will my idea actually work?', 'How can I build a solid venture around it?', 'Will I find an investor for my company?' or 'How will I get my first few customers?'

Which is why I decided to write this book. To dispel myths and misconceptions about entrepreneurship and, at the same time, to give youngsters a good idea about what it takes to set up a venture and then scale it up profitably.

While a few books on entrepreneurship have already been written, this one is specifically about student entrepreneurs – ordinary young Indians who are doing something extraordinary. By setting up their own ventures in their twenties, they have become CEOs; something most others take years to achieve, if at all. Which I why I call these youngsters 'The Underage CEOs'. They are pursuing their own vision and making a difference to their chosen domains. Most importantly, in spite of all the challenges and pressures, they are having the time of their lives!

This book is mainly about the journeys of eleven student entrepreneurs chosen from the big cities and small towns of India. Not one of them has studied in an IIT or IIM. All of them have graduated from lesser-known institutions. Yet they have not let this come in the way of their entrepreneurial dreams.

Towards the end of this book, there are a couple of insightful interviews – one with a leading investor and another with an entrepreneur who raised funds not long ago. Also in this book are the key points your business plan should address.

I hope this book gives you a flavour of what entrepreneurship is all about. I hope it answers a lot of your asked and unasked questions and helps you realize that entrepreneurship is not just about madness, but also about method.

But more than anything else, I hope this book gets you to shed your inhibitions and fears, and get off the starting blocks immediately. It must make you blow your cheeks and say, 'Oh, boy! Why the hell am *I* not doing something like this!?'

Happy reading! And happy starting up!

How Have the Entrepreneurs Been Chosen for this Book?

As you flip through these pages, you will meet an eclectic bunch of youngsters. They are some of the best young entrepreneurs from across India. While they come from diverse backgrounds and have different personalities, all of them have a few important things in common.

So, here's why they have made it to this book:
- The youngsters featured here did not become entrepreneurs by chance or because someone forced them. On the contrary, they *chose* to strike out on their own.
- All of them resisted pressure from friends and family to strike out on a different path.
- They have opted to become 'career entrepreneurs'. Which means that they took the plunge right after college with practically no corporate experience.
- All of them are running early-stage ventures. Which means that their experiences are all fairly recent and not something that happened a long time ago. That makes the situations they faced and their decisions relevant to you.
- Each of them has a big vision for his/her company.
- None of them see entrepreneurship as a means to get rich. In fact, their focus is not on amassing personal wealth, but on generating wealth for a larger group (their employees, vendors and other associates).
- Each one of them is setting up an organization. None

of these youngsters wants to run a one-man show.
- Each one of them is keen on making an impact in the market/customer segments they are catering to.

A few of the ventures featured here took birth in small towns. This just highlights the fact that in these times, you can set up a venture in any kind of place. There are opportunities everywhere.

While some of these ventures have been founded by men, others have been founded by women. And finally, I have tried to choose a good mix of industries/business domains.

It is wonderful that many youngsters are seeing a profitable business opportunity in the so-called 'social sectors' like education and environment.

Writing This Book – My Journey

Writing a book is a journey in itself. A very personal journey of exploration and discovery. In writing about these entrepreneurs, I ended up discovering a lot about myself!

I clearly recall the dark, cold night when I boarded a bus to meet the first entrepreneur I would profile for this book. As I pulled my jacket around myself, sipped a cup of scalding hot tea and watched the rain come down in fat pellets, my mind was on the long journey that lay ahead. I knew it would be tough to write this book while also holding down a full-time job. Still, I was confident that I could manage it.

Scheduling appointments with entrepreneurs living in different cities, meeting them to understand their life stories, reading up on contextual knowledge and then actually writing the book involved a lot of logistical jugglery. There were times of maddening delay when I felt that things were simply not moving ahead.

But the best part of writing this book has been meeting the entrepreneurs and chatting with them and their teams.

Two things kept me going through it all.

One was the belief that these entrepreneurs (and several others like them across India) are doing something remarkable at such a young age. I wanted to chronicle their fascinating stories and present them to a larger audience.

The other was the unflinching support of my family, friends and associates. Like I have said somewhere in this book, getting the support of family and friends can make all the difference to an entrepreneur. And to me, it *did* make all the difference in writing this book – which too is an entrepreneurial journey of sorts.

As you read the stories that follow, it will be good to keep the following points in mind:

- By and large, I have not disclosed the financial details of each venture – like revenue, profit and size of investments – because they are confidential in nature. Also, I think they are not as important as the stories themselves.
- There is no universal definition of ambition, success or failure. It is up to each entrepreneur to decide what his/

her goals are and then decide whether or not he/she has succeeded in the pursuit of those goals. In fact, going by their sheer grit, resourcefulness, drive and vision, I would say that *all entrepreneurs* are successes.
- The stories in this book indicate what is happening across India, in big cities and small towns. As you read this book, several other college students are quietly foraying into the 'start-up life'.

1. WEB SCHOLARZ
KOLKATA

Founder: Sourav Karmakar
Name of the company: Web Scholarz LLP
Nature of business: Online information security solutions – mainly training and consulting.
Founded in: 2014
Based in: Kolkata
Team size: Six
Vision for the venture: Building a company which will meet the internet and data security needs of this generation. We are focussed on creating values and ethics in the business of cyber security.
URL: http:www.webscholarz.com

Sourav Karmakar's story is the modern-day equivalent of 'Alice in Wonderland'. In the original fairy tale, Alice dives down a rabbit hole and opens a door to find herself in a wonderful garden. In Sourav's case, he tapped a few keys on his computer, jumped over a few (fire) walls and voila! He found himself inside somebody else's computer!

Sourav's profession has a magical quality. A layman is likely to be mesmerized by it. As an ethical hacker and cyber security specialist, Sourav is part of a new-born industry. He is part of a small group of specialists who are shaping the contours of this industry in India today.

Here is the story of how he chanced upon the world of cyber security, and how he is building a profitable business in this domain.

What the Hack!

Sourav Karmakar meets me on the pavement near his office. We shake hands, after which he leads me up a flight of stairs to his new office. I find a number of cubbyholes and desks all packed inside. Practically every inch of space has been utilized. We find ourselves a comfortable corner and sit down. Chai in hand, we start talking.

I learn that Steve Jobs and Jack Ma are Sourav's role models. Steve Jobs for his clear vision about what his products should do for people, and Jack Ma for his jaw-dropping metamorphosis from an English teacher to China's most inspirational business tycoon. Sourav has closely followed the lives of both these giants and has learnt a lot from them.

Sourav was lucky that his life-defining moment came very early in life. When he was in Class 9, he started fiddling with his friend's computer and learnt about the Internet and its super possibilities. But the 'wow!' moment for him came while watching *Die Hard 4*. The concept of a 'fire sale' cyberattack was a revelation to him. He'd never imagined that it was possible to hack into traffic signals, banks, gas and transport systems of a city, and bring them crashing down in a matter of minutes. This was his first glimpse of hacking. Mesmerized, he started reading up about it. He had to search high and low on the Internet and collect information from various sources. Over the next few days, he greedily drank in as much information as possible on the subject. And he was hooked!

He understood that hacking into information systems was a whole new world, but most people in India knew nothing about it. If you knew the art and science of hacking, the computer could literally become a toy in your hands.

Excited like a child, he now wanted to test his newfound knowledge. With further help from Google, and a few failed attempts later, he managed to hack into the Orkut accounts of a few people. Thrilled to bits, he tried to learn how to hack into mobile phones, databases, etc. Also, he learnt about the different kinds of viruses and malware that could affect computers.

From the moment he got his own computer at home, he started spending even more time on the subject. He visited the websites of companies that were in the business of online information security and found that there was an 'ethical' side to hacking too. An ethical hacker is a computer and networking expert who systematically tries to penetrate a computer system or network on behalf of its owners. His/her intention is to find out the security flaws that a potential hacker could exploit, and to fix them. Sourav was especially fascinated by YouTube videos which explained the subject in graphic detail, complete with demos.

In 2009, Sourav reached Class 12. In that crucial year, he had to pay more attention to his studies and couldn't spend much time on his true love – hacking. But one particular incident from that year is clearly etched in his mind. It is the memory of watching the English film *The Core* which showed many aspects of hacking. He particularly loved how the guy hacks into the mobile phone network and makes calls free of cost to any place on earth! 'I am so tickled by that scene even now,' laughs Sourav.

After his Class 12 board exams, he wrote the AIEEE and IIT-JEE, but fared poorly in both. Knowing he would not get admission into any good institute, he decided to take a year's break and prepare for next year's JEE. He enrolled himself in a coaching institute in Kolkata. For all of that year, Sourav travelled from Chandannagar (where he lived) to Kolkata (where the coaching classes were held) and back every weekday. He might have been physically present in the coaching classes, but his mind was on – what else! – hacking.

Through the week, he would grit his teeth and somehow sit through class. And come Friday, he would rush back home gleefully, itching to log on to his computer. But since the BSNL dial-up connection at home was painfully slow, Sourav would recharge his mobile phone with an Internet pack and use that to access the Internet over the weekend. No surprise then that he ended up going back to class on Monday with most of his assignments unfinished! 'Every Monday, I used to promise myself that the *next* weekend, I would study for the JEE and focus only on my assignments. But that never happened!'

Soon he had accumulated a hard disk full of technical videos, tutorials and articles on hacking, cyber security, cryptography and other related topics. That year passed in the blink of an eye and it was JEE time again. This time too, however, he did not score well in the entrance exam. Obviously, he was disappointed. But because his score in the West Bengal Joint Entrance Exam was good, he gained admission to the B.P. Poddar Institute of Management and Technology. Funnily enough, he was happy about the admission because the college campus had free Wi-Fi and every student was given a laptop by the college!

As his journey of learning about hacking continued, Sourav realized that one had to be strong in the fundamentals if he/she wanted to master the subject. The problem was compounded by the fact that he was learning all this by himself, with the Internet as his only teacher. He would have learnt things better and faster if he had found a good training institute.

Interest in hacking was high among the students of his college. When Ankit Fadia, a well-known hacker, came to their college to address the students at a seminar, a large crowd turned up to listen to him. The audience seemed mesmerized by the world of hacking and it seemed a very cool thing – magical and mystical.

Sourav was taken aback when he learnt that Ankit had been paid Rs 1 lakh for the seminar. The huge turnout of students and the fact that Ankit had been paid a large sum of money for just a few hours of work told Sourav that there was a big business opportunity in this field. And because there were hardly any training institutes that taught this subject, there seemed to be a big gap in the market. It was a gap that Sourav wanted to fill as early as possible.

As the first step in that direction, he decided to give himself and his knowledge of hacking a little publicity. He started a blog on the subject and kept posting on it regularly and promoted his blog on Facebook. One day in February 2011, during his second semester in college, the brother of a friend called him up and started asking him a lot of questions on the subject. As he was talking to this person (Abhishek Banerjee), Sourav sniffed an opportunity. He convinced Abhishek to speak to the principal of his college and get permission to organize a half-day seminar on hacking. Sourav said he would give the students a glimpse of the fascinating world of a hacker and charge only a nominal amount.

Abhishek spoke to the principal, who gave permission to hold the seminar. Sourav was on!

About 260 students attended this seminar. Sourav remembers being a little nervous since it was his first one ever. And it was not a small crowd! But soon after he started talking, he lost himself in the subject. He managed to hold the attention of the audience throughout his sixteen-hour talk and answer all their questions too. When the session ended, Sourav was physically drained, but on an emotional high. Going by feedback from the audience, he could call his first seminar a success. What's more, he had earned his first income. The college had fixed Rs 175 as the attendance fee per student for the seminar. Of the total income generated, the college kept half and gave Sourav the rest. All things considered, Sourav earned a reasonably large amount of money that day. That too by talking about a subject he loved and knew well. He was so pumped up! He now wanted to take on more such seminars.

Facebook helped him to promote himself further. Slowly word spread in Kolkata, Chandannagar and other areas nearby about his knowledge of hacking. After a while, his own school (Desh Bandhu Memorial High School, Chinsurah) contacted him and requested him to conduct a seminar for its students. The principal said that hacking seemed to be a cool, new thing and asked if Sourav would teach the children the basics of the subject. Sourav gladly agreed. And so it was that he conducted his second seminar in November 2011.

As the number of calls such as these increased, Sourav also heard questions like, 'Sir, what's the name of your company?', 'Do you provide any certification to your students?' or 'Where is your office?' He realized that the absence of a proper training infrastructure could soon become a stumbling block because it would limit his capacity to conduct training programmes. And if he could not offer certification to the people he trained, that would reduce the appeal of his programme too. Whatever course they undergo, people always look for a certificate at the end of it, something they can flaunt to get a job or projects.

Sourav understood that he shouldn't keep operating as a one-man army, conducting training programmes for colleges. He should move to a more professional, more corporate level.

Now, that meant he would first have to take a close look at hacking the industry, not hacking the subject. There is a difference between the two. Understanding the industry would mean identifying the needs of the average consumer, the infrastructure needed for a training institute, the legal and financial aspects of setting up a business, etc. From the Internet, he learnt that Innobuzz, a Delhi-based company, had a training centre right next to his college campus! He met the manager of the training centre posing as a student and extracted details about the institute.

He found that the institute charged Rs 8000 for their course on online information security. The course covered twenty-two topics. But the funny thing was that Sourav knew eighteen of them already! Or so he thought. He decided to enrol in the course during his summer break (after Year 1 of engineering) and test his knowledge. Acting ignorant of the subject, he attended classes throughout his summer vacation. He found that his earlier assessment of his knowledge had been right – he knew all but three topics that were taught in the course. And those three topics were quite advanced – Wi-Fi hacking, exploit writing and buffer overflow.

During the course, Sourav would keenly observe the faculty members and students. He noted the questions asked by the other students and the way in which the faculty members answered them. He himself posed questions to faculty members to test their knowledge of the subject. He thought that the institute was not doing justice to the subject. It was covering various topics in a cursory manner, not going deep into them. Some students realized it and were disappointed while others did not even realize it.

Since Sourav's idea was to set up his own training institute at some point of time in the future, he decided that his institute would offer students a lot more knowledge on the subject and equip them really well.

The itch to get into business was strong. Back in college, he discussed his desire with Sunny Raj, a college mate. Sunny was always talking about business and looking for opportunities to earn money.

Getting into the training business would mean having an office (even if it were a small one) and the necessary IT hardware and software. Also, they would have to prepare high quality study material. Where would the money and people for all this come from? Sourav definitely didn't want to ask his parents for money. He couldn't take a loan from a bank either because he had already taken an education loan to study engineering.

He was in a fix. He came to know of a company called Cybercure Technologies, an institute that offered courses in online information security. Cybercure wanted to expand its base in the West Bengal market aggressively and was keen on conducting more courses there. Sourav contacted them to ask if he could be a campus ambassador for them. He said he could arrange for Cybercure to conduct training programmes for college students. He would speak to college managements and secure permission for the training programme. A trainer from Cybercure would then come over and teach the students. The cost of travel for the trainer and the cost of preparing the study material would be borne by Cybercure. Sourav had to bear the boarding and lodging expenses of the trainer and the marketing costs incurred. He proposed that he would take 40 per cent of the total fee collected from every training programme. Cybercure could keep the rest. The institute liked the idea and agreed.

For a change, Sourav thought he would contact college students directly instead of going through colleges. In other words, conduct open programmes in which any college student could participate. His logic was that this method could turn out to be cheaper – a rough calculation told him so. He could conduct the programme at a low-rent venue and hire a projector and screen for the duration of the training. This way he could pocket the entire profit accrued instead of sharing it with the college management.

And so he decided to arrange for a two-day 'open' programme as a trial and see how it panned out.

Scouting for a suitable venue, he was shocked when private venue owners asked for Rs 20,000 to Rs 25,000 per day for a moderate-sized hall! After an intense search, he finally managed to find a venue owned by the Municipal Corporation of Bidhannagar for Rs 7000 per day. This was a manageable sum. He could cough up the money by borrowing some from his parents and taking some from the five friends who were partnering him in this effort. Next, to promote the seminar and attract participants, he tried something interesting. With the help of his friends, he approached various colleges and roped in one student per college. These students were given the role of commission agents. That is, they had to get other students of their college to participate in the seminar. For every confirmed participant he/she brought in, the student would get Rs 100. That was the deal.

It worked! However, it took some intense selling on their part over the next few weeks. They used a combination of several methods to reach out to college students – emails, phone calls, Facebook posts, posters at colleges, etc. They managed to get 123 participants for the seminar, charging a fee of Rs 1000 per participant.

And now came an 'ouch!' moment for Sourav. After the programme ended, he found that his team had made a profit of Rs 25,000. This meant Rs 5000 per head. A paltry sum, he thought, considering all the time and effort they had invested into the seminar.

Sourav realized that he should either ask for a higher share of the profits for the next programme or set up a training institute himself.

His resolve to set up a company of his own strengthened. Training would be one of the services his company would offer, he thought. But before setting up his own company, he wanted to work for some time in one that was already in this field. After talking to a number of people, he met Christy Mathew through Facebook. Christy was working for Tech Bharat Consulting LLP, a company that offered consulting services in online information security to companies. Christy asked Sourav to visit their head office in Delhi for an interview, to which he happily agreed.

But he hadn't anticipated his parents' reaction to his decision to go to Delhi. When they heard about it, they threw a fit. 'They said that until then, I hadn't gone out of West Bengal at all or travelled alone anywhere! How would I make it to Delhi and back all by myself?!' Sourav recalls with some amusement. Repeated attempts to convince them did not work. Finally he borrowed Rs 4000 from a friend and on the eve of Holi, left for Delhi. Without his parents' permission. He didn't like it, but felt that there was no other way. In Delhi, another friend agreed to put him up. Sourav attended the interview at Tech Bharat, passed it and was appointed as a trainer for east and south India. Since he was a college student at that time, Tech Bharat told him he could conduct training programmes when he was free. He would not be on the rolls of the company as a full-time employee.

For the rest of that year (2012), he conducted seminars on hacking in thirty-five or forty colleges.

All this while, Sourav kept in touch with his contacts in the information security industry (like the Black Hat

Communities and other fora), keeping himself informed of the trends and developments in the industry.

Apart from being a trainer for Tech Bharat, Sourav was also conducting training programmes and seminars on his own – as a freelancer. He had also taken tentative steps towards consulting. Interestingly, one of his earliest clients was none other than the Kolkata Police! One day in 2011, Sourav was poking around the website of the Kolkata Traffic Police as a part of his R&D efforts. He found some security vulnerabilities on the site and reported this to the police. At first there was no response. After 2 months, he got in touch with an officer of the Bank Fraud Department in the police and reported the matter to him. He then got in touch with a few senior officers of the Lal Bazaar Police station of Kolkata who called Sourav over for a meeting. He met them and gave them a full download of the security problems of the police website. He helped them fix the issues too.

From that time onwards, the delighted and grateful police officials have been calling him in as a consultant on their online security matters. In 2011, he was given the 'Commissioner's Award', for Cyber Crime Agencies for helping them solve important cases of cybercrime.

In July 2012, Sourav, Ankur Biswas and Surajeet Ghosh came together to set up their training and consulting company. They named it SAS Securities. The letters 'SAS' stand for the first letter of each of their names. Reluctant to invest too much money at that stage, they registered the company as a proprietorship in their names. They agreed that Sourav Karmakar would take charge of technology and marketing, Surajeet Ghosh would be the business head and Ankur Biswas, the head of finance and sales.

In August 2013, Mr Murali Sharma, a senior IPS official, asked Sourav to train his team of cyber detectives. This team was called Cykop. Sourav trained them over eight consecutive weekends in certified ethical hacking and computer forensics investigation. The cops were in a curious position because Sourav trained them to hack into their own computer network to detect vulnerabilities. They were then taught how to strengthen the security of these networks. They learnt penetration testing, hacking web servers and services, social engineering DOS attacks, sniffing attacks, evaluating electronic crime scenes, steganography, log management and other such arcane stuff. The detectives were asked to discuss their cybercrime cases in light of what they learnt in this programme.

This was the first training programme conducted by SAS Securities. The fact that it was run for the police made it extra special for Sourav and the team. 'We were happy that the first programme was for a good cause, something that would help society. By training the detectives, we made them better at solving cybercrime.'

Happy with the training programme, the Cykops spread the word about SAS Securities to their colleagues in other departments and units. Soon, the West Bengal CID contacted Sourav, asking him to train some of its officers in the detection and prevention of cybercrime. Then came the Bidhannagar Commissionerate. Next, it was the turn of the Barrackpore Cyber Cell. By this time, SAS Securities had acquired quite a reputation within the police circles. They felt that apart from having a deep knowledge of the subject of information security and hacking, SAS Securities was a reliable partner – someone who would keep sensitive crime-related information highly confidential.

SAS Securities conducted three more training programmes for colleges until April 2013. As of 31 March 2013, the company's turnover was Rs 13 lakh. It was not a bad figure at all, considering that they had reached it in their first nine months as a company. They knew that for the first two years, their focus had to be on building the right image, a solid reputation in the market. Which meant that it was fine to have only a few assignments, but each assignment had to be executed extremely well.

In April 2013, Sourav completed Year 3 of engineering. One more year in college and then he could jump into business full-time! That month marked an important personal milestone because he informed Tech Bharat that he was leaving them. He wanted to spend more energy and time on SAS Securities and nurture it along with Ankur. Tech Bharat was sorry to see a good trainer go, but they also understood his entrepreneurial ambitions. They wished him well and let him go.

In May 2013, Surajeet Ghosh, one of the three founding partners of SAS, left the company. He got a job offer, which he accepted. He got married recently, and had a few important family commitments. Hence the decision to take up the job. His departure affected Ankur and Sourav because Surajeet had helped their R&D work immensely, using his experience and technical skills. However, he assured them that he would be available to them for help and guidance.

At that time coincidentally, Ankur and Sourav realized something funny, though important. They saw that they were getting a number of calls from people asking them to send them watchmen and security guards! The entrepreneurs were flummoxed. Why should people call *them* for watchmen? Mulling it over, they realized that the reason lay in the name of their company ('SAS Securities')! They promptly decided to change it to SAS LAB Technologies Pvt. Ltd and applied to the Ministry of Corporate Affairs accordingly. Their application for a name change was accepted and they heaved a sigh of relief. Slowly the calls asking for watchmen reduced!

From one of his friends, Sourav came to know of an organization called Electronic Commerce Council (ECC), which was based in the USA. It offered a certificate in ethical hacking. Sourav and Ankur read up about the company on the internet and asked a couple of friends who were in the ethical hacking profession about it. They learnt that ECC's certificate was valued highly in the industry and found that they could become an Accredited Training Centre (ATC) of ECC by paying Rs 1.85 lakh per annum. This would allow them to become an authorized training partner of ECC and offer the ECC international certification.

A friend analysed keywords used on Google (that is, those related to hacking and online information security) and found that 'certified ethical hacking' was one of the top terms people searched for. Checking with a few people, they found that IT companies like TCS, Cognizant and Capgemini give a lot of importance to international certification. Employees who hold certification are likely to get better roles and performance ratings.

Convinced that there was a lot of demand for such certification, SAS Securities signed on as one of the ATCs of ECC for east India. They paid the annual fee, partly from the company's revenue and partly from Ankur's personal funds.

Having obtained the accreditation, they mentioned this fact on their website and added 'certified ethical hacking' as a keyword in their Search Engine Optimization (SEO) efforts. The traffic to the site shot up to 10,000 in a period of eight-nine months. Apparently, a lot of people out there wanted to be certified ethical hackers!

June 2013 was an important month for SAS Labs because it got its first three students for the Certified Ethical Hacker course.

When SAS Labs signed on with ECC, they received ten certification kits. They had to sell all the kits in a year because the ATC status itself was valid only for one year (after which it had to be renewed by paying the annual fee again). The fees for the ECC-accredited training and certification was Rs 30,000. But since this was a large amount, what if they did not find many takers for it?

So Sourav thought they should offer a more affordable certification course as well. After a few discussions, Ankur and he decided to offer another version of training and certification for Rs 10,500. This version did not include certain advanced topics that were part of the ECC certification course.

Their decision to go with ECC paid off – their feel about the market had been right. In their first year of being an ATC, they sold twenty-two kits – twelve more than the mandatory ten! Since the margin on these programmes was reasonably high, the company made some decent money through them.

Between April and December 2013, SAS earned a revenue of Rs 25 lakh, which was nearly double the revenue it earned in the first nine months of its existence. The icing on the cake was a training contract from a top MNC (all the details about this deal are highly confidential; I am not even allowed to reveal the client's name!). This just goes to show the power of consistently chipping away at the market and building your reputation – one training programme at a time. The ECC accreditation also helped considerably.

'2013 was a good year for us. We learnt a lot. Also, that year we got the feeling that our company became somewhat stable in terms of operations. Finally, our revenue grew a lot too!'

2013 was also the year Sourav got a job offer from Cognizant Technology Solutions through campus placement. For obvious reasons, he rejected the offer and moved on, intent on building his own enterprise.

In December 2013 came another turning point. He participated in the Global Student Entrepreneur Award conducted by the Washington-based Entrepreneurs' Organization. He emerged a runner-up in the competition. At this event, he met Rajesh Kankaria, an investor. Rajesh expressed interest in investing in SAS Labs. Sourav and Ankur went to his office and discussed the matter with him. Rajesh said that he found a lot of potential in their line of business and so, would like to invest some money in their company. Further, he said he would help them get more business using his network of contacts. In return, he wanted a certain stake in the company.

Sourav was all for it because he believed Rajesh would add a lot of value to the company. But Ankur did not agree. He did not want to dilute his stake in SAS; instead he asked Sourav to sell his stake in the company to Rajesh if he wanted. Sourav felt this was unreasonable. He thought that both partners should sell an equal portion of their respective stakes and make the deal go through. The disagreement went on for some time, with no resolution in sight.

At this point of time, a couple of well-meaning friends and elders asked Sourav to walk out of SAS Labs and set up another company. Even Rajesh Kankaria and Pramod Maloo (another entrepreneur whom Sourav had met recently) advised him to do the same thing. Their logic was that if the co-founders disagreed on some fundamental issues and had personal differences that they could not resolve, it was better for one of them to move out of the company and start a new venture.

Should Sourav decide to set up a new venture, Rajesh said he was willing to invest in it. He offered to provide Sourav with the necessary infrastructure and give him a monthly allowance of Rs 10,000 with which to pay the employees.

Pramod Maloo too offered to invest in the new company. Pramod runs a company called Kreative Machinez which offers website development, SEO and digital marketing solutions to companies across the world. He said that Sourav and he would be equal-stakes partners in the new venture. Further, he said that Sourav could access the entire set of Pramod's current and past customers, and try to offer online information security services to them. In one shot, that would give Sourav access to 230 companies!

Sourav found Pramod's offer better and took it. Still, the decision to walk out of SAS Labs was an extremely difficult one. SAS Labs had been his baby. Walking out was like abandoning that baby to an uncertain fate. It took a lot of time for him to be convinced that it was the right decision. Discussing the matter with a few close friends helped him think clearly and decide.

On 2 June 2014, Sourav's final year engineering exams ended. On 5 June, he started working for his new venture, which he and Pramod decided to name Web Scholarz. Sourav and Pramod decided that Web Scholarz could share office space with Kreative Machinez, Pramod's existing company. Pramod shifted four of his team members from Kreative Machinez to Web Scholarz. This gave Web Scholarz a big boost – the fledgling company acquired the capability to handle projects right away.

With the office available and the team ready, Sourav and Pramod invested some money in marketing Web Scholarz. They contacted all the colleges for which they had earlier done workshops and offered to run training programmes for them again. Quite a few colleges agreed. This time they ran the programmes on Skype. It took the team a whole month of non-stop work to prepare comprehensive training modules and toolkits.

Meanwhile, Sourab Das (a close friend of Sourav's from his college days) started publicizing Web Scholarz in the USA and directed prospective customers to their website. Sourav started approaching Pramod's old set of clients. He explained to them that Web Scholarz was a partner company of Kreative Machinez and that it offered online training programmes and cyber security services such as penetration testing, server load balancing, malware removal, setting up intrusion detection systems, etc. Would the client be interested in any of these services?

Now, cyber security is rapidly emerging as a priority for most companies across the world. With the amount of malware floating around on the Internet and the number of phishing attacks, the threat to online information is very high. And so, companies are keen to take the necessary security measures and protect themselves.

Using this approach, Sourav and Pramod managed to get quite a few projects. Some of the companies they acquired as clients were USA-based companies like Valley Anger Management, The Dioz Group and Industrial Safety Products (ISP). The fee ranged from Rs 30,000 (for a one-time scanning of flaws, recommendation of security protocols and systems, followed by a three-month warranty type service) to Rs 1 lakh (for a year-long project which included full scanning twice a month and an automated monthly report on their IT systems).

All this while Sourav had continued to consult with the Kolkata Police and a few other companies on a freelance basis. He informed all of them that he had set up Web Scholarz. They all wished him luck since they liked Sourav's competence and professional attitude. They believed that the kind of work he was doing was very valuable to a number of organizations. He had therefore acquired a lot of goodwill over the years.

In a curious twist of fate, Sourav's work for the Kolkata Police on a particular case helped him find another investor for his company. Someone had hacked into the computer network of Mr Siddharth Jain's mining company and had stolen confidential customer data. When Sourav helped the police solve this case, Mr Jain was happy and enquired about Sourav's business. Sourav explained it to him in detail and said that he was looking for funds to scale up Web Scholarz. Mr Jain, who also owns an investment company, saw growth potential in Web Scholarz and decided to invest some money.

Sourav has come a long, long way from the time he accidentally chanced upon the world of hacking. Today he is a reputed consultant and trainer in cyber security with his own team of specialists. He, his partner Pramod and their team are helping companies secure their valuable information assets, giving them total peace of mind. They work closely with the police to solve criminal cases too.

Sourav and Pramod have big plans for Web Scholarz. They want to move the head office to Delhi, which has far more business potential than Kolkata. Also, they hope to open an office in Dubai soon, to tap the Middle East market.

Here's hoping that Sourav continues to have a 'hack' of a journey!

Sidelights

- Sourav loves riding his bike in the silence of the night. Often, he takes off on long rides with his friends.
- He calls himself a 'vampire in the world of computers' because when the world is asleep, he is awake, digging into computer systems.

Sourav's Message to Young Entrepreneurs

- Your college degrees and other certifications are not your skills. Always go after real achievements from your hard work, experience and failures. What you learn through your passion are your real skills.
- Get out of your comfort zone. Like a child, be ready to experiment and do unusual things. Don't be afraid to fail.

Key Learnings from Sourav's Story

- It is very important to listen to your intuition – your gut feel. This tells you what you really want to do at various points of time. Many successful entrepreneurs often follow their intuition. They end up making better decisions and feel happier about them.
- In business (or even in life in general), there is no substitute for depth – that is, the pursuit of excellence in any subject. Stay curious forever and keep learning. This attitude will help you tremendously.

2. Add-on-Gyan
Manipal/Bengaluru

Founder: Priyadeep Sinha
Name of the company: Add-on-Gyan Educational Services Pvt. Ltd
Brand names: Gyan Lab, Kidovators
Nature of business: Hands-on, activity-based practical education for school children; a resource portal for parents; a platform for identifying the most innovative ideas of children.
Founded in: 2011
Based in: Bengaluru
Team size: Eight
Vision for the business: To reach out to ten lakh school children by 2021. And to open a school that solely follows this unique learning method.
URL: www.addongyan.com

Priyadeep has an insatiable curiosity about everything in the world. This curiosity makes him ask the most basic (yet often forgotten) questions – what, how, why, who, when and where? Not surprising then that he has founded a company whose central purpose is to feed the curiosity of children and to stimulate a sense of wonder and discovery in them.

Priyadeep comes across as a person who has his head firmly placed on his shoulders and feet planted on the ground. He believes that true entrepreneurship means doing something original and not following the herd. As he (with his team) goes about building his young company, he knows that there is much more at stake than just business growth or profits. His venture is a trendsetter. It has the potential to change the Indian school education system, which has so far been based on rote, rote and more rote.

It is this realization of the power of his idea that keeps Priyadeep thinking about his business idea night and day.

'Other companies make software, soaps, aeroplanes, etc. We aim to make great human beings.'

CHILD'S PLAY

Priyadeep Sinha's clear eyes are smiling at me from behind his spectacles as he delivers this statement. He couldn't have summed up the purpose of his venture in a more succinct manner. For Add-on-Gyan does exactly that by providing a simple yet effective method through which school children can learn various concepts. This method helps children get a practical understanding of whatever their teachers have taught them theoretically in the classroom. Which also explains the choice of the name for their company. In Priyadeep's opinion, his venture tries to add on to the gyan (knowledge) children have already acquired in the classroom. Just that, the child acquires this 'add-on' gyan in a hands-on manner.

Add-on-Gyan's delivery model is this – the team has identified several topics/concepts/questions across subjects like humanities, social sciences, maths, physics, chemistry, biology and life skills where they believe that a practical way of learning can enhance the children's grasp of the topic or concept. They have created simple and practical activity kits to illustrate and explain each of these topics/concepts.

Here are some of the concepts for which activity kits have been created:
- Metal detector
- Area and perimeter
- Movie projector
- Two-way switch
- Water level indicator
- Cloud formation
- Time zones of the world
- Eco-friendly lanterns
- How to withdraw money from a bank
- How to pay taxes
- How the parliament functions

Each concept is brought alive with the help of activity kits. Using them, children learn how to build a metal detector or understand the meaning of the term 'perimeter' or the different time zones of the world. In a trice, a metal detector or a movie projector is transformed from a vague, abstract term to something that the child has built with his/her own hands. Children are, therefore, able to understand the ins and outs of the concept much better and are able to relate to its meaning, its working and its importance.

These curricular activities are delivered under the name of 'Gyan Lab', which the company has trademarked. A Gyan Lab typically comprises a room, some simple furniture like tables, chairs and storage shelves and the demonstration kits built around various concepts. However, more than the room or the other items, the name 'Gyan Lab' stands for a whole new approach to learning. It is an approach which recognizes that 'learning by doing' is a powerful and necessary corollary to 'learning by reading and writing'.

Simple, right? That is why the idea of Add-on-Gyan is so powerful. Any idea that recognizes a distinct and neglected need or gap in the market and addresses this need in a simple and effective manner is sure to have a far-reaching impact.

'How did you hit upon this idea?' I ask Priyadeep.

'I have the habit of spotting problems in daily life and trying to figure out a solution for them. The idea for Add-on-Gyan came from this habit.'

Priyadeep understood that one of the chief limitations of the Indian education system is its emphasis on rote-based learning. From kindergarten to Class 12, and even through college, children are goaded to learn their lessons 'by heart' and then regurgitate them during exams. This, they are told, is a sure-fire way to score well and ensure their admission to higher classes. Never mind that they do not know the practical relevance of a concept or they can't even visualize it properly. It is enough that they memorize what is printed in their textbooks, and which their teachers faithfully repeat from those very textbooks in class. For years, our education system has been running in this manner. Such an approach to education leads to some serious problems:

- Children become like blinkered horses. They take a straight and narrow view of life, learning not to question or probe deeper into whatever is taught in classrooms. As a result, their innate sense of curiosity and imagination is stifled very early in life. When curiosity and imagination are lost, creativity is killed.
- When this happens at a nationwide level, you have a country where institutions and companies are run largely by left-brained thinking (in other words, logical/ rational thinking). There is hardly any room for right-brained (or creative) thinking. And so, as a country, we do not come up with much disruptive thinking, innovations, original discoveries, etc. At least not as much as we should.

This is a fundamental societal problem that India faces. One that Priyadeep and his team have taken on through Gyan Labs. They have realized that the solution to this problem is to intervene in the early phase of a child's life. In other words, at the primary and secondary school level.

This is the time when the child's mind is being moulded. A period when the child will be highly receptive to whatever is being taught to him/her.

Gyan Labs are meant for students from Classes 4 to 9. They have been created inside the campuses of existing schools. Priyadeep and team approach schools and explain their concepts to the principals and senior teachers. A few forward-thinking schools have already signed up with Priyadeep's company to set up Gyan Labs in their campuses. In the first full commercial year of the company, twelve Gyan Labs were set up in places as diverse as Manipal, Kota, Pune, Bengaluru, Hyderabad, Kundapur and Mangalore.

It is apparent that a lot of effort must have gone into developing and fine-tuning the business idea before it was formally launched.

It seems like a good moment in the conversation for me to ask Priyadeep about how it all began; how he took his idea to the market and commercialized it. Priyadeep takes a deep breath and goes into flashback mode.

In 2010, Manipal Institute of Technology (MIT), where Priyadeep was studying mechanical engineering, organized a business plan competition. Eager to participate, Priyadeep thought furiously about the business idea he should work on. He wanted to spot one that would be simple and, at the same time, would address a deep-rooted need in society. After hours spent mulling over this matter, he hit upon the subject of education and the chief limitation of the Indian education system (learning by rote). Drawing from his own experiences in school, he decided to do something to address this problem. That is how he arrived at the idea of providing a much-needed practical education method to primary and secondary school students, thereby feeding their sense of curiosity and helping them go beyond theoretical learning.

Priyadeep and his batchmate Abhash Kumar wrote out the business plan together and submitted it. To their surprise and delight, their plan won! And the duo was richer by Rs 60,000. At around the same time, they came to know of a similar event called 'Provenance' being organized by the Manipal University Technology Business Incubator (MUTBI), an in-house venture incubator set up by their university. Nine winning business ideas would be chosen at the event and incubated by MUTBI. They would also be offered other assistance like access to funding and mentoring. Priyadeep recalls that he was confident of his business plan doing well. 'However, I did not know whether we would win or not. The only way to find out was to participate.'

Their business plan made it to the final round. The panel of judges had five members. Four of them were sceptical about this idea. One of them even said that something similar had been tried by NCERT and had failed to take off. However, the fifth judge saw potential in their idea. He felt that by tweaking the plan here and there, it could be made to work. In any case, he felt it should definitely be tested. In the end, this was one of the nine winning business ideas and they were told that they could now get their idea incubated at MUTBI, if they so wished.

The students who had submitted the other eight business plans backed out because they wanted to take up jobs. To them this had probably been just another competition by winning which, they could have earned some money. Or maybe they thought they had good ideas and just wanted to test the strength of those ideas through this competition.

In any case, the Priyadeep-Abhash team was the only one that decided to actually take their business plan to its logical conclusion. They accepted the offer to get incubated by MUTBI, thereby creating local history. This was the first student-led enterprise to come out of MIT in sixty years! It was a moment of supreme achievement and joy for the duo. This significant event was to set off a chain reaction, inspiring other students of MIT to become entrepreneurs over the next few years.

And so, in January 2011, the venture was registered with the incubator. Priyadeep and Abhash started work from a two-seat cubicle. Like in so many other cases, the seed capital for the venture came from family. Over a period of time, Priyadeep's dad had accumulated a sum of Rs 1.5 lakh in his savings account. Knowing that this amount would make a big difference to the venture his son was trying to set up, he handed over the entire sum to Priyadeep. The young entrepreneur was overwhelmed by this spontaneous gesture, something he feels emotional about even now.

With some money in their kitty now, Priyadeep and Abhash heaved a sigh of relief and promptly set about fleshing out their business idea and developing the activity modules they had envisaged in their business plan. At this stage, the team was bolstered by Sonali's entry. Sonali, who was a collegemate of Priyadeep's, joined the founding team in February 2011.

Developing the activity modules took a full two months and involved lots of reading and several rounds of intense discussions. Developing activities for school kids meant that the entrepreneurs had to 'become' kids themselves. They had to pore over the textbooks prescribed by different schools and put themselves in the shoes of children! After going through the textbooks with a fine-toothed comb, they had to identify topics/concepts for which the practical activity modules could be developed. The idea was to pick topics which were somewhat abstract or difficult to grasp through theory alone. 'That way, the child would derive greater value from our practical exercises,' explains Priyadeep.

After the initial set of topics was chosen, the next step was to actually procure the raw materials and assemble some sample kits for the activities. Getting the right materials was vital. 'We wanted to use materials that the kids could handle easily. Only then would they enjoy creating various things with those materials. Also, the materials had to be durable since children would be using them extensively.'

Getting the right materials proved to be an arduous task. Priyadeep and Sonali scoured several online business directories and contacted more than a hundred manufacturers before they found the kind of materials they wanted. As they started assembling the kits, the entrepreneurs felt a sense of elation. Their dream was slowly, but steadily, taking shape. At the same time, Priyadeep couldn't help rueing the fact that such a method of learning had not been available to him when he was in school. If his generation had had the benefit of such a hands-on method of learning, it would have learnt so much more!

At around this time, the team cracked the name of the company and the brand name under which they would set up activity centres. At the same time, another important realization dawned on them. Given that they had no corporate experience, they thought it would be vital to have a 'worldly-wise' person as their mentor. This person, they felt, would be very useful in guiding the venture and shaping its evolution. He/she could also leverage useful connections in the industry.

Enter Mr Chandrashekar ('Shekar Sir' to Priyadeep and his colleagues). It was Shekar Sir's suggestion that the team should pilot the Gyan Lab concept in a school. This meant going to a school and setting up a 'test' Gyan Lab, building some sample activity kits and allowing the school's children to use these kits. This would tell them how their concept of an activity lab worked under real-school conditions and what changes/adaptations would be needed to make the lab more effective. If the lab's model had to be tweaked in any way, it was better to do it right then, rather than try to do it after setting up many labs.

Shekar Sir helped them get in touch with a school that was part of the Manipal K-12 chain of schools. They laid out their test lab there (the Manipal K-12 chain of schools was set up by the Manipal Educational Group in association with a company called Tutorvista). As expected, the pilot lab threw up a lot of learning pertaining to the choice of activities, the choice of materials, etc. In fact, many new activities were identified during this phase. Also, the pilot exercise gave the team a good idea of the space and storage arrangements needed for the lab and its materials.

At the end of the pilot phase, the promoters' conviction in the power of their idea grew. They were fairly clear that in Gyan Labs, they had a robust, scalable idea. They could set up these labs in schools all over India if they wanted to.

I mull over the model they created for Gyan Labs and realize that it is very simple and modular. The space needed for each lab (approximately 250 to 300 sq. ft) comes from the school in which the lab is being set up. The school is also asked to provide some shelves where the lab's materials are stored along with some tables and chairs for the children. Add-on-Gyan has to ensure that the right kind of materials are procured and stored safely in the lab. Each lab involves anywhere between 9000 and 25,000 material components. Ensuring that these are procured at the optimal price and quality, and ensuring that they are used and stored properly is important. Thanks to the labs, the Add-on-Gyan team is learning a lot about logistics and inventory management!

And oh! There is one other key element that the company has to take care of when setting up each Gyan Lab. An element that actually brings the concept of Gyan Lab alive and makes it work. And that is the human element, in the form of a lab coach. The lab coach is a facilitator who sets the lab sessions in motion, observes the children's activity and gently guides them as and when necessary. The coach is instructed and trained not to demonstrate any activity to the kids, but to let them learn by themselves using pictorial aids. The core objective of a Gyan Lab is to make the children think for themselves and learn purely through trial and error. If a child has a serious doubt, the lab coach asks a senior student to help out, thereby making peer-to-peer learning possible.

The company selects its lab coaches carefully. The key criterion for selection being that he/she must enjoy being with kids and must be able to handle them well. 'A coach should become the children's friend in no time,' says Priyadeep with a grin. This aspect is vital because unless the coach is able to understand children and interact with them at their emotional level, he/she cannot get them to open up and actively participate in the activities.

At this point, I was curious to know more about Mr Shekar and his contribution as a mentor to the organization. I wondered if roping someone in as a mentor had indeed been valuable for the company. I put the question to Priyadeep and was surprised when he got a little emotional. It turns out that bringing Shekar Sir on board as a mentor was one of the best things that could have happened to the fledgling venture. A well-rounded person, Mr Shekar had helped a dozen start-ups. His experience in handling issues that a start-up would typically face has been invaluable to Add-on-Gyan. Somewhere along the way, the company added two other senior professionals as advisors. Mr Luis Miranda, co-founder of HDFC Bank and Dr Kusum, academic head – Pearson Schools, joined hands with Shekar Sir to guide the company through key matters. Priyadeep's dad, Mr Pulak Sinha, who works with the State Bank of India, is the financial advisor to the company. He has regular discussions with Mr Shekar and Luis, helping the company navigate the waters.

Priyadeep's respect for these four seniors was evident in the way he talked about them. He and his team consult them on every important aspect of the business. Not just that, they also use the seasoned veterans as sounding boards for new ideas and initiatives they want to implement.

'Our mentors have been our backbone. They are sound professionals and our most ardent evangelists. Our relationship operates purely on the basis of mutual trust. I am grateful that they have agreed to help our venture out.' The mentors' interest in the company's development is so great, that when the company faced a cash crunch, they came to the rescue. The large sum of money they lent the company from their personal funds helped it tide over the crunch.

My next question to Priyadeep was about the size and composition of his team. I learnt that one year from the inception of the venture, Abhash withdrew from it. While he had been deeply involved in setting up the venture, he decided to pursue a career in journalism. Fortunately though, his involvement with the company did not stop just because he moved out of it. To this day, he continues to champion the idea of Add-on-Gyan and actively promotes it.

Priyadeep's team has seven members apart from himself. Astoundingly, the average age of the team is just twenty-three years! Each member of the team has taken charge of a specific aspect of the business. For instance, Sonali, who has been designated chief technology officer of the company, is in charge of developing the activity kits, testing them and ensuring that they adhere to certain standards. Priyadeep calls her the most creative member of the team. Another member focuses on interacting with suppliers, placing orders for materials and tracking their delivery. While the 'senior' members of the team take care of higher-level activities like interfacing with schools and parents, developing the curriculum and kits, taking strategic decisions, etc., the junior members mostly take care of operational tasks.

Helping the team is a bunch of interns – most of them recruited from Priyadeep's college. Having interns is a good idea. On the one hand, it gives a bunch of eager-beaver college students the chance to learn the operations of a business practically. On the other hand, for the company it is a cost-effective way of getting work done. Also, the company can very likely spot a spark in some of the interns and recruit them as full-time employees.

A chartered accountant, a company secretary and a lawyer help the company with financial, legal and statutory matters. This is something the core team of employees is not equipped to handle. It makes sense for the core team to concentrate on managing and building the business while matters like law and finance are taken care of by specialists.

I am impressed at the professional and systematic manner in which Priyadeep has gone about setting up his team and company. It is not often that one sees entrepreneurs employ a high level of rigour in their venture. More often than not, they tend to build things 'on the fly', which means that many things are done in an *ad hoc* manner. Priyadeep and Sonali don't fit into this stereotype.

Priyadeep and Sonali are keen to achieve steady, profitable growth. They are the kind of people who value quality more than quantity. They are therefore prudent in deploying funds. So far, Add-on-Gyan has won cash grants at the Dell Social Innovation Challenge, the Dell Education Challenge and the Power of Ideas. While the first two events were conducted in the USA, the last-mentioned event is annually conducted by the *Economic Times* in association with the Centre for Innovation and Entrepreneurship, IIM Ahmedabad. The Technology Development Board and the Ministry of Micro, Small and Medium Enterprises (MSME) of the Government of India have also recognized the importance of Priyadeep's idea and awarded grants to Add-on-Gyan. The cash grants have all been ploughed into the venture to facilitate growth.

Today, Add-on-Gyan is cautiously expanding. In an intelligent move, it has added two new initiatives to its basket of offerings. Apart from adding revenue streams to the venture, the two new initiatives have helped the company de-risk itself by reducing its dependence on Gyan Labs. The new initiatives are:

1. A competition called Kidovators for school students. This is a platform for encouraging children to think up innovative concepts in science and technology, thereby spurring them to push the frontiers of their mind. The first edition of Kidovators, held in December 2013-January 2014, saw 25,000 students from across India participate. The best 150 were invited to Bengaluru for the finals. Prizes worth Rs 12 lakh were given away. The second edition of Kidovators was held in January 2015 and attracted 27,000 participants.
2. A resource portal for parents (GyanLab.com). This portal provides parents with a wide range of relevant information and advice on bringing up children. While a few parent-centric portals are already present in the market, Priyadeep and team think that they do not give parents any advice or counselling on bringing up kids the right way. This is the gap GyanLab.com is trying to fill. 'In just fifty days after the launch, we have got about 9000 people on this portal. Every day, about forty questions are being answered on a one-to-one basis by our counsellors.'

At the same time, the company is also trying to make Gyan Lab kits and sell them to parents.

Priyadeep and his teammates are keen to live up to the expectations of their customers. And so, ensuring that all their offerings work very well is of critical importance to them.

Priyadeep is confident that his young and enthusiastic team will make it big. The entire team knows that their company is doing something that is of primary importance to the Indian economy.

In that sense, Add-on-Gyan is not just any other venture. It is actually a movement in the making.

Sidelights

- Priyadeep lives in his office so that he can always be close to work. Work keeps him on a high all the time. So much so that he doesn't feel the need for other stimulants!

Priyadeep's Message to Young Entrepreneurs

- The life of an entrepreneur, especially one who takes the plunge at a very young age, is tough. An entrepreneur therefore needs to be disciplined and should intensely focus on the venture he/she is creating.
- Do not crave instant gratification; be ready to wait for the rewards.

- Do not build companies for investors, build it for your customers. If you can create value for your customers and they are willing to pay well for what you are offering, you can run your company on 'bootstrap mode' for a long time.
- Try your best to get your parents to support you in your start-up effort.

Key Learnings from Priyadeep's Story

- Business ideas are present all around you. In fact, you only have to closely examine your own experiences and problems to spot a few super business ideas. Priyadeep's idea was inspired by his dissatisfaction with the teaching methods used in his school.
- Before you formally launch your venture, do your homework thoroughly. Priyadeep, Sonali and their team members spent a few months testing and building their business model bit by bit before they commercialized their venture.
- Consider hiring bright interns. They have the right attitude and can be moulded to work the way you want them to. Most importantly, they won't cost you a bomb!

3. GharPay
Hyderabad

Founders: Arpit Mohan and Abhishek Nayak
Name of the company: GharPay Technological Services
Brand names: GharPay, ClinkNow
Nature of business: GharPay is a door delivery and cash payment collection service for e-commerce businesses. ClinkNow is a platform that banks can use to offer targeted deals and bargains to their customers.
Founded in: 2011
Based in: Hyderabad
Team size: Fourteen
Vision for the business: To simplify payment mechanisms and help people get more meaningful deals.
URL: www.gharpay.in (this has now been linked to the Delhivery website) and www.clinknow.com

GharPay Technological Services has had an interesting trajectory so far. It was founded as a company that offered consumers a simple way to pay for their e-commerce transactions (someone would come to your doorstep and collect payments for the product/service you had bought online; the name GharPay says it all). After numerous ups and downs, it grew in revenue and expanded its footprint across India.

And then, in September 2013, it sold its offline payments collection business to Delhivery, a company that provides logistic solutions for e-commerce companies. After the successful sale, the GharPay team moved on to developing a software named ClinkNow. It is an electronic platform or network that uses customer-purchase data sourced from banks to help advertisers find consumers who would be most receptive to their brands.

Read on to see how the GharPay team built up this venture, scaled it up and then successfully exited the business at the right time.

CONVENIENCE. HOME DELIVERED.

For the past decade or so, e-commerce has grabbed a lot of attention from Indian investors as well as the media. After the dot com bust at the turn of the last millennium, a second wave of e-commerce companies emerged a few years ago. This time they had better business models, spotted new needs and opportunities to tap and built better infrastructure. Soon enough, investors started eyeing this second coming of e-commerce with interest.

E-commerce quickly grew to become the darling of the Indian entrepreneurial movement and was feted by the media. Companies like MakeMyTrip, Flipkart, Snapdeal,

Groupon, etc. have emerged as the stars in the firmament of e-commerce in India.

While the nation's attention was riveted on the trajectories of these companies, another story was quietly playing out on the sidelines. The story of those companies which had made use of the opportunities created by the growth of e-commerce in India. The smarter ones grabbed the coat-tails of the fast-growing e-commerce movement to script their own growth stories. GharPay was one such company.

Abhishek Nayak and Arpit Mohan, the founders of GharPay, graduated from Birla Institute of Technology, Pilani (BITS). While Arpit graduated in 2010, Abhishek did so a year later. The idea of GharPay was born in Abhishek's fertile mind.

During his time at BITS, Abhishek Nayak dabbled with different non-academic projects, including a few not-for-profit initiatives. 'I didn't want to be restricted by the academic curriculum of my program. I wanted to learn much more than that. And BITS gave me many opportunities to do so.'

Abhishek was doing a five-year programme in his college. By the time he reached the fourth year, he realized that he was thoroughly confused about what to do professionally. 'I didn't know what I should do in my career. I was clueless,' he said. After thinking about it, he decided to take a semester's break from college and do something else during that time. The idea was to take a break from academics, clear his head and give himself some time to think about what he wanted to do.

Landing a job as a research analyst at Bloomberg in Hyderabad, Abhishek spent a very interesting six months in the city of Charminar. His job at Bloomberg involved sifting through loads of data, making sense of it and then preparing concise reports from it. While the job itself was not so interesting, his time in Hyderabad was. He met a lot of people from different walks of life – entrepreneurs, activists, students of economics, business leaders, youth leaders, etc. Hanging out with such people opened up his mind. It exposed him to different ways of thinking, to different world views. Some of the people he met were Europeans. And it is from them perhaps that Abhishek learnt his biggest life lesson. Which is, people should set their own priorities in life and set timelines for themselves.

'Many Europeans do not let themselves be bound by the goals and milestones that society has traditionally been setting for individuals – like getting a job, reaching the top of the hierarchy, getting married, having children, etc. A lot of them decide what they want to do in life and when. This really blew my mind,' said Abhishek. This moment of epiphany helped him set his priorities for the next decade or so. Abhishek decided that he would not get into the rat race that life is for most people, especially Indians. He decided to try his hand at a few things on his own and see where that led him.

Returning to BITS after a six-month gap, he completed his course. During this time, his mind went into overdrive, thinking of what kind of venture to start. Ideas were a plenty, but the key question was which one to choose.

I ask Abhishek how he evaluated each idea, how he decided which ones to discard and which ones to pursue. He says that he tried to follow a logical process to evaluate them. After hitting upon an idea, he would write down the problem that idea was supposed to solve. This became the problem statement. He would then figure out, in some detail, how the idea would work as a solution to the problem. The next step would be to talk to potential customers, those who were facing the problem and who were likely to opt for the solution Abhishek was building. The point in talking to potential customers was to understand if he had approached the problem correctly and whether the idea would solve it. Further, it helped him understand if the idea was realistic or if it was fraught with difficulties. Working out the economics of the business idea and the various systems and processes it called for (like sales, payment collection, conflict resolution, etc.) was the final step in the evaluation of the idea.

I am impressed. One doesn't find many people who evaluate ideas scientifically. Abhishek apparently believes in doing his groundwork thoroughly before investing more energy, time and money in an idea.

One of the people he would bounce each idea off of was Arpit Mohan, his senior from BITS, who was working in Hyderabad. During his stint at Bloomberg, Abhishek had been able to spend a lot of time with Arpit, discussing his ideas and plans for the future. Arpit too was feeling the urge to become an entrepreneur. He thought he would join hands with Abhishek if a good idea came along.

The idea of GharPay was the eithteenth business idea that occurred to Abhishek. At first, he rejected it because he thought it was an operations-intensive model. However, as time passed, he found that he couldn't get away from this idea. He discussed it with Arpit. They evaluated the idea again and found that the market need for it was strong. A very real problem could be solved if they could build a suitable solution. They thought they would hire people with the right experience to help them run the company.

The market scenario as they saw it was like this – e-commerce was growing steadily in India, a number of companies had come up in the past few years and were selling a wide range of products. From train and flight tickets, hotel rooms, books, electronic gadgets, furniture and furnishing to clothes and cosmetics. Why, even diapers were being sold and bought online. Many online retailing companies had a growing customer base and a high brand recall. These companies had tied-up with courier/logistics companies for the delivery of the products to the customer's doorstep.

Several online retailers had started offering a Cash on Delivery (COD) service. This meant that you could order a table or a book on a particular website and opt to pay cash when the product was delivered to your doorstep. You therefore did not need to pay online using a credit card, debit card or Internet banking. Offering COD helped online retailers expand their customer base considerably since even those who could not pay online could buy a host of products. COD was touted to be a game changer in the business of online retailing. It was expected that the COD part of e-commerce businesses would grow rapidly in the years to come.

Abhishek and Arpit realized that fundamentally, there were two kinds of products being delivered by online retailers – one, 'physical' goods or cargo (like cushions, furniture, shoes, clothes, etc.) and the other, 'virtual' products like train/bus/flight/movie tickets and coupons (with discounted deals and special offers). The bigger courier companies were more interested in delivering physical products (since they could earn higher rates from those). They were not interested in delivering low value items such as tickets, discount coupons and the like, mainly paper products.

The two entrepreneurs thought there was a business opportunity for a new player in offering a COD service for these virtual products. They could tie up with online retailers like redBus.in, BookMyShow.com, Groupon.co.in Cleartrip.com, etc. and deliver their tickets and coupons to customers. Delivering these products was relatively easy. Also, it did not call for huge investments from the company. The company would not need warehouses to keep the paper products, it would not have to manage an inventory of goods and finally, the risk of damage or loss in transit would not exist.

This was the idea of GharPay. This was chosen as the name of the company for obvious reasons – customers would pay when they received the product at their doorsteps. (In Hindi, the word 'ghar' means 'home'.)

To find out if this idea was indeed a feasible one, Abhishek and Arpit spoke to a few e-commerce companies they knew. Their research validated their assumptions about the COD business in India – 1) it was growing fast and 2) there was a need for reliable partners for delivery and cash collection.

Charged up by these findings, the friends set up GharPay in January 2011. Arpit quit his job at Kony Labs and joined the start-up as co-founder. The seed capital came from their parents. Between the two of them, the youngsters had borrowed Rs 5 lakh. Much of this money was invested in renting an office, hiring the first set of executives and building an in-house order management system.

The fledgling company got its first order from redBus.in, an online retailer of bus tickets.

For a player in the COD business, the key is to earn the trust of the online retailers it wants to tie up with. It has to give the retailers confidence that the money collected from customers will be handled well and that the correct amount will be handed over to the retailers without any glitch or delay. GharPay was keen to earn the trust of redBus.in and demonstrate that it was a reliable and efficient partner. Only then, the founders knew, would they get other customers.

Abhishek sent an email to Phanindra Sama (Phani), co-founder of redBus.in, asking if he wanted to outsource the delivery of redBus' COD orders. Phani replied, saying that nearly 20 per cent of redBus' orders were taken on

COD basis and that the company was indeed looking for a reliable firm to which it could outsource the COD deliveries and cash collection. Phani agreed to sign up with GharPay for a trial period of three months and then evaluate their performance. It was mutually agreed that depending upon the performance over those three months, the contract would either be terminated or extended.

Arpit had the honour of delivering the first set of tickets. He remembers going around Hyderabad on his motorcycle, making deliveries to customers and collecting cash from them.

I ask Arpit and Abhishek what kind of IT system they built to manage their orders since tracking deliveries and cash collection in real-time is extremely important for this business.

Arpit tells me that to begin with, they built Application Programming Interfaces (API) so that they could integrate GharPay with the online merchants on their checkout page itself. Next, they built a dashboard that would allow merchants to track their orders on a real-time basis. The billing and invoicing automation solution was the last piece of the jigsaw. Once that was done, GharPay had a complete order management system which was built in-house with Arpit being the key driver behind its development.

And what about their first team, I ask. How did the entrepreneurs find their first set of teammates? Arpit continues the narrative. He admits that hiring the first set of executives for the company was not easy. He and

Abhishek were keen to find the right people, especially because they themselves had no experience in this business. They wanted to recruit at least a few people who had worked in the logistics business earlier. The more important thing was to find those with integrity and the right mindset. 'Finding people for a start-up is always difficult. We can't offer much money, at least initially. Also, there are thousands of things to be done, the workload is very heavy.'

The founders hired people through others they knew. This guaranteed that they were hiring individuals with the right skills, background and mindset. Right from the beginning, Abhishek and Arpit paid attention to their team. Their teammates, though young, are by no means naïve. All of them are articulate and rational and believe in doing their best for the company.

In the blink of an eye, the trial period given to GharPay by redBus.in was over. It was evaluation time! A lot depended upon what the redBus team felt about GharPay's performance in Hyderabad. They looked at GharPay's on-time delivery record, turnaround times, service levels and the ability to fulfil orders, and they found that their performance had met their expectations. RedBus.in was ready to not just extend the contract for Hyderabad, but also award a new territory, Chennai, to them.

Arpit, Abhishek and their teammates were elated! The extension of the contract and addition of another territory was a thumping endorsement of their reliability and efficiency. 'The extension of the contract boosted our confidence. Since we had no prior business experience, winning the trust of our first client was vital to our success,' says Arpit.

GharPay set up an office in Chennai and hired a team there in order to serve the market well.

Apart from redBus.in, GharPay's other initial customers were Nathella Jewellery, MeraEvents.com and Crazeal.com, which was the earlier version of Groupon. In their sales pitch to a prospective customer, the GharPay team would highlight the real-time nature of their order management system and their performance record over the first few months after starting up. To some of their prospective customers, they even had to sell the concept of COD itself, telling them that the customer base could grow if they started offering this payment method.

To all their customers, GharPay guaranteed that the product (ticket or coupon) would be delivered to the buyer's doorstep within twenty-four hours from the time of purchase. The company signed a Service Level Agreement (SLA) with each of its customers. The SLA guaranteed that the cash collected from buyers would be transferred to the online retailer's account and reconciled in the system within forty-eight hours of the buyer paying the money.

Soon after GharPay had established themselves in Hyderabad and Chennai, investors started noticing this small company operating in an interesting niche. Sequoia Capital was among the first investors to express interest in GharPay. Arpit and Abhishek first met Shailesh Lakhani of

Sequoia in December 2011 in Mumbai at a start-up event and kept in touch with him over the next few months. One day, Shailesh told them to formally approach his company for investments. Arpit and Abhishek, who were definitely looking for external funding to help them grow faster, were delighted.

They met a team from Sequoia in May 2012, explained their business, presented their plans for growth and pitched for investments. Arpit and Abhishek's mentor, Raju Reddy helped them present a strong case to Sequoia. He had been mentoring GharPay since its inception. He had been an entrepreneur himself and was closely involved with the BITS Alumni Association (BITSAA) and The Indus Entrepreneurs (TiE). People considered him to be a good mentor.

Sequoia liked what they saw and agreed to invest in GharPay in return for a stake in the company. A fortnight after this meeting, they signed a deal with GharPay and agreed to pump in USD 3,00,000 to fund the company's expansion.

The entire GharPay team was overjoyed! Bagging this investment was definitely the high point in the short life of their company. With this infusion of funds, the company could invest in more people, set up branches in other cities and upgrade its technology. It could also offer better salaries to its team; it would not have to penny-pinch any more. A big relief indeed!

This deal was followed by a dizzying expansion phase. In just four months, GharPay expanded its footprint from two cities to six. It added Visakhapatnam, Delhi/NCR, Bengaluru, Pune, Mumbai and Kolkata to its network. In each city, Arpit and Abhishek had to find the right office space, install their order management system, hire the right people and train them – all in rapid succession. It was a breathless time for the small company.

I comment that such rapid expansion is not common even among big companies and that it must have been a testing time for GharPay. 'Oh, yes! And the most extraordinary phase too!' replies Abhishek with a grin. The entire team went through tremendous pressure during this phase. Tempers frequently ran high as the teammates argued about every key decision. Being young, articulate and opinionated, each member of the team wanted to do things their way.

To their credit, they never let these situations get out of control. 'At all times, we knew that we had to work as a team if the company was to succeed. So, even if we had strong opinions on everything, we learnt to give and take. We learnt to work with one another's strengths and weaknesses.'

Apart from the speedy expansion, another reason the team struggled during this phase is that they had had to set steep targets and goals for themselves because they now had Sequoia on board. Having an investor with them also meant constant evaluation, something the GharPay team was not prepared for. This put additional stress on them.

To my mind, this was the toughest phase in their story. Yet, this was also the phase that taught the team the most. Truly, it was trial by fire.

Once GharPay had expanded across India, it added more customers to its list. Companies like Jet Airways, Cleartrip.com and BookMyShow.com had become their customers.

Soon though, Abhishek and Arpit realized that their business was facing some serious problems. The growth in their revenue had slowed down considerably. They went back to their initial calculations about the business and pored over them for days. They also read up a lot on what was happening to e-commerce in India. To their horror, they realized they had overestimated the market potential for their business. Not by a small degree, but by as much as five times or more! In other words, the true market potential for their kind of business was only one-fifth of what they had originally estimated.

This was a serious problem. They thought furiously about bringing the business back on the growth path. After several discussions, it seemed clear that one way out was to expand their scope of service to include the delivery of all kinds of products (like CDs, furniture, clothes, etc.) and collect cash against the delivery. This would however entail investing in warehousing, inventory management and a superior order management system. Also, the risk in the business would rise manifold. The team was not ready for any of this.

For almost the whole of 2012, GharPay went through great uncertainty.

During this time, Arpit and Abhishek kept thinking of other business ideas as well. One day they came up with the idea of developing a peer-to-peer (P2P) payments solution. Arpit calls it 'something like Whatsapp meeting your bank account'. The product, which they subsequently named Zap, was very simple. Using Zap, I could choose my friend's name and number from the address book on a smartphone and send him or her money. That's it. The money would be transferred immediately from my account to my friend's. Unlike online banking, one did not have to add the friend as a beneficiary.

Zap was mainly meant for the young, urban crowd which is tech-savvy and uses the smartphone a lot anyway. People in this age group would love to pay their bills and borrow/return money to friends through Zap. They would simply love the convenience this solution offers them.

Arpit and Abhishek spoke to a few people and understood that they would have to sell Zap to banks, which in turn would sell it as a service to its account holders. Being a payment solution, it had to be routed through banks. When they met a few banks and explained the product to them, they seemed interested in it.

The entrepreneurs promptly put together a team and started to build Zap. While the technical team of GharPay, headed by Arpit, was involved in developing Zap, the company also recruited two more people to beef up the design team. These were people who had some technical experience in developing a payment solution.

Some time later, their product was ready. However, no bank was ready to actually buy it. Arpit and Abhishek found that all banks in India, especially the nationalized ones, have a labyrinthine process for buying products. It is not easy to become a vendor to a bank.

In this case, there was another reason for the delay. Though they had expressed some interest in Zap earlier on, the banks did not find this product good enough to buy immediately. They did not think their account holders would find this product exciting and buy it in large numbers.

GharPay had hit a wall a second time.

As all this drama was unfolding, the COD part of GharPay's business kept moving ahead, though somewhat sluggishly. In October 2012, the company managed to raise a second round of capital – mostly to fund the development of Zap, though it was decided that a small part of this money would be used to support the COD business.

In November 2012, five months after they had first pitched Zap to a few banks, GharPay grew tired of waiting for them to actually buy the product. The team was disappointed that the banks did not appreciate the true potential of this simple product. Still, there was no point in moping around and waiting forever. They had to decide their next step. In their heart of hearts, they knew that they now had to think of *yet* another strategy to revive their company – that is, they had to change course again.

Arpit, Abhishek and their core team (comprising colleagues Rachit and Roshan) went back to the drawing board. They sought advice from their mentor Mr Raju Reddy as well as their investors. Coming up with another idea was not easy. The mood in the company was understandably low, given the difficulties of the past ten months. All of them knew they had to come up with something really good in order to put the company back on the growth path.

If necessity is the mother of invention, I'd say desperation is the father.

From interacting with many banks over the past few months, Arpit and Abhishek knew that these banks had surplus money to invest, but were slow to adopt new products and technology. This is why they did not latch on to Zap quickly. They saw Zap as a nice-to-have product, not something that would fetch them high returns. Or even as something *their* customers needed immediately. And so, GharPay had to come up with an idea that the banks would be very keen to buy into – something that they would need urgently.

During one of their discussions, the issue of debit cards came up. They discussed the fact that a while ago the RBI had set a ceiling on what is known as Merchant Discount Rate (MDR) for debit card transactions. MDR is the amount charged by a bank from a merchant outlet such as a shop or restaurant for transactions made using a debit or a credit card. The recent RBI ruling asked banks not to charge an MDR of more than 0.75 per cent of the value of any debit card transaction. In effect, RBI capped the revenue a bank could generate from its debit card user base. Ever since the rule came into effect, the only way a bank can earn more from its existing debit card users is by pushing up their transaction value.

But how can a bank get a debit card user to make transactions for a higher value? This is where ClinkNow came into the picture.

ClinkNow, a product devised by the GharPay team, was a software which would help a bank analyse the purchase patterns of its debit card users in an anonymized fashion. By using ClinkNow the bank would come to know if a particular customer was buying more shoes, music CDs or short-duration holiday vouchers (he would have to buy this last item online from a website like Groupon.in). The bank could then sell this data to merchants – online and offline – and help them send customized messages and offers to the debit card user about the products he was buying often. This way the debit card user may be tempted to buy more from the merchant, pushing up the merchant's revenue from that particular user. As for the card user, he/she wins too, since they get deals and discounts on products that they are interested in.

Arpit and Abhishek discussed this idea with their colleagues, mentor and investors. They spoke to a few banks to get their opinion too. In the end, it did seem like an idea worth pursuing. They thought ClinkNow's time had definitely come. The excited teammates turned their combined focus on creating it.

Developing this product called for a lot of money and undivided attention. Arpit and Abhishek felt they could not concentrate on ClinkNow and, at the same time, run the operationally-intense COD business.

The die was cast. They decided that it would make sense for them to exit the COD business. If they could sell it to a company that was interested in logistics/cash collection, they could plough the sale proceeds into ClinkNow and fully concentrate on developing and marketing their new product. The entire team at GharPay felt that this was the right way to go.

And so in July 2013, GharPay sold its COD business to Delhivery at a good valuation. Delhivery is a logistics company that wanted to add offline payment collection to its range of services. The deal made sense to both parties. GharPay channelled the money earned from the sale into ClinkNow.

There was a sense of immense relief in the team. They felt they could now look towards the future and develop ClinkNow, which they saw as a new-age product.

The youngsters did face a few challenges in developing such a product since the team did not have prior experience in developing banking software, especially one that performed data analysis. They therefore hired a couple of knowledgeable people to help them develop this product.

ClinkNow was successfully piloted in a few banks and got a positive feedback from them. The team then managed to sell the product to other banks as well.

In June 2014, there came another high point in their journey. In a déjà vu moment, ClinkNow was acquired by a Bengaluru-based company called Ezetap. While ClinkNow was involved in transactional marketing data, Ezetap made POS machines like credit card readers. The synergy between the two businesses was good enough to convince Arpit and Abhishek that Ezetap would be a good home for ClinkNow. They felt that at Ezetap, ClinkNow would get more resources and better attention than it would have at their small start-up.

It has only been a few years since they set up GharPay, but Arpit and Abhishek have lived an entire lifetime in this short span of time! They are happy that they set up two different businesses, created value in both and finally, sold both at good valuations. They are confident that the companies that have acquired GharPay and ClinkNow will nurture both brands and take them to greater heights.

They give full credit to their teammates, who stood by them throughout and always made the company's well-being their top priority. Says Arpit, 'With this team, Abhishek and I can enter any business and succeed.'

Their mentor Raju Reddy has had a big hand in guiding them. Right from their days in college, he has been a steadying influence on them.

It is very likely that the two youngsters will think of another business idea soon and commercialize it.

As the axiom goes, 'once an entrepreneur, always an entrepreneur'!

SIDELIGHTS

- Abhishek and Arpit love board games. They have several of them – Settlers of Katan, Carcassonne and Puerto Rico – at home.

- Some time back, Arpit and Abhishek went to meet a bank manager to pitch Zap, their mobile payment solution. The manager, who turned out to be from Orissa, told them that he would listen to them only if Abhishek – who is from Orissa as well – made the entire pitch to him in Oriya! Abhishek did so in broken Oriya, leaving Arpit somewhat dazed and amused.

Arpit and Abhishek's Message to Young Entrepreneurs

- Build products that people desperately need.
- Test every assumption you make – about the market, consumers, competition, pricing, etc.

Key Learnings from Arpit's and Abhishek's Story

- Evaluate your business idea thoroughly before you decide to move ahead with it. Critically crunch some numbers to get the right estimate of the size of the opportunity you are looking at. Speak to some of your target customers, investors and other senior industry people to get their feedback on the idea. This will help you tweak and strengthen your idea or ditch it (if it is wide off the mark).
- To the extent possible, hire people for your company through people you know. That way, there's a better

chance that you'll find the kind of attitude and profile you want.
- Try your best to build a great culture in your company. It is easier said than done, but it is vital for the sustained growth of any company. A great culture will ensure that people have fun while doing great work and that they have a strong bond with the company.

4. iKheti
Mumbai

Founder: Priyanka Amar Shah
Name of the company: iKheti
Brand name: iKheti
Nature of business: Setting up and maintaining sustainable urban farms.
Founded in: 2012
Based in: Mumbai
Team size: Eight
Vision for the business: To create a platform for individuals and communities to grow healthy consumable crops within their premises, and to promote sustainable urban farming.
URL: www.ikheti.co.in

Eager-beaver and a lover of nature and animals, Priyanka's story is proof that your family background and upbringing have a big hand in shaping your worldview and approach to life. Born into a family that loves animals and nature, Priyanka has chosen to tread a path that seems so natural and so *right* to her – though to the outsider, the vision she has chosen for herself can seem a little daunting!

In the vast concrete jungle of Mumbai, Priyanka is sowing the seeds of a quiet revolution. A green revolution, if you will. Will she be able to change the mindset of city slickers and bring back a beautiful, earthy concept that has all but vanished from the urban landscape over the years?

Read on to understand how Priyanka is building a profitable venture in a domain that has been crying out for attention for a long time.

Your Home Is Your Garden

Mumbai. A city with a human population of two crores. A city which has one of the highest population densities in the world. For decades it has been the engine of India's economic growth. Here real estate has been more precious than gold (figuratively and sometimes even literally) for many, many years. Where buying a 500 sq. ft pigeonhole of a flat is difficult for many people.

It is in this overpopulated urban jungle that the good old kitchen garden (if you don't know what that is, ask your parents!) is trying to gain a toehold. And it has found a champion in Priyanka Amar Shah, the founder of iKheti.

iKheti was born over a casual dinner-time conversation in late 2011. At that time, Priyanka's college, Welingkar Institute of Management, Mumbai, was organizing a concept show called Dmagics. As part of the programme, every participant had to come up with a business idea, flesh it out by writing a business plan and then present their plan to a panel of judges. The judges included investors, senior working professionals and other experts. The idea was to foster entrepreneurial thinking in the students of the college. Priyanka signed on for it.

Over dinner one night, her brother Rahul said, 'Why don't you help people grow kitchen gardens?'

'The idea seemed so logical and so apt for me, considering my upbringing. I took to it immediately,' says Priyanka, recalling that life-changing moment. It was logical and apt because Priyanka had grown up with a kitchen garden at home. Her parents used to grow lemons, chillies and curry leaves in their flat and use them in their cooking. She thought to herself that if her parents could maintain a kitchen garden in the limited space available in their flat, then so could the others who lived in similar apartments across Mumbai.

A kitchen garden (or 'urban farm' as Priyanka calls it) promises quite a few benefits. It provides you with your private green area (your lung space) at home. It makes available chemical-free vegetables right at home, thereby reducing your dependence on the vegetable market.

Also, by 'farming' small vegetables and herbs at home, you are bringing the farm-to-plate distance down to zero. Which is an environment-friendly move on your part for two reasons. One, there is no wastage because of transportation. Two, as there is no transportation involved, the carbon footprint of the home-grown food is zero. Finally, there is the cost element. By eliminating the cost of transportation and the commission payable to agents all along the food transportation chain, you save a bit of money too!

At a deeper level therefore, a kitchen garden encourages people to learn and practice a simpler and more sustainable lifestyle.

As a person who loves nature, the idea appealed to Priyanka. 'I thought this would be a very good thing for a city which is so full of concrete and so devoid of plant life. I wanted to build a profitable business out of this idea.'

Priyanka decided to present the idea at Dmagics, the concept show. But first, she explained the idea to her faculty mentors in college and asked them what they thought about it. At first, they were somewhat taken aback – 'Farming? And in the cramped houses of Mumbai! But where is the space?' was their first reaction. Upon hearing this, Priyanka showed them a few pictures of the plants her family had actually grown at home and explained that they would not take up much space at all. The clincher was the fact that many planters could be mounted on walls and even hung from the ceiling! They are widely used across homes in America and Europe.

When her professors saw the pictures, her idea started to make sense to them. They were surprised that a good bit of ingenuity had gone into the design of a home farm. They discussed the idea amongst themselves and realized that it was possible to make a viable business out of it after all. They therefore selected it as one of the business ideas that would be presented to the panel of judges at Dmagics.

Taking this decision as a pat on her back, Priyanka and two of her classmates started doing the necessary groundwork to back up her idea. They began to build a robust case for a sustainable venture. She knew that the judges would ask a lot of questions; it would not be easy to convince these seasoned veterans of the viability and scalability of any idea.

Priyanka decided that the first step would be to get a clear understanding of market realities.

She knew that people usually bought plants from neighbourhood nurseries. In our large urban sprawls, nurseries are primarily the only places which sell plants to people – unlike in many other countries where they are widely sold in retail outlets and malls too. Over the next few days, Priyanka visited a number of nurseries across Mumbai for a first-hand feel of what they offered. While at the nurseries, she spoke to a few customers as well and some interesting facts came to light:

- By and large, all nurseries sold decorative and flowering plants. People bought them mainly to decorate their houses, to bring in that aesthetic touch which comes only with having plants at home. Others kept them for the fragrance from the flowers or to offer those flowers to God.
- The only edible plants sold by nurseries were tulsi, pudina, ajwain and kadi patta.
- The pots were earthen or plastic (which was acceptable), but of poor quality (which was not!). The earthen pots would crumble easily; also, over a period of

time there would be fungus growing on them, making them difficult to maintain. Not having been glazed and finished properly, they had a very kutcha (raw), rough-hewn look. The plastic pots, on the other hand, were not eco-friendly and looked tacky.
- Plant-selling was a highly fragmented and unorganized activity across the city. Nursery to nursery, there was no consistency in the quality of the plants. Besides, every nursery sold pretty much the same range too.
- But the most important finding came from Priyanka's conversations with the consumers. Knowing that a large majority of people did not keep plants at home (even if they had space to spare), she wanted to find out why. To her surprise, she found that deep down people *did* want to keep plants at home. They liked plants and enjoyed being close to them. However, a lack of knowledge (about what kind of plants to keep, how to nurture them properly, how to maintain them, etc.) was a big problem for them. Not only did they know very little about it, they also didn't want to make the effort to learn!

To me, this mindset is an indication of the extent to which people have become alienated from nature. They have been migrating from villages to cities over the last few centuries in search of jobs and in pursuit of their dreams. The shine of lucre is, after all, much brighter in cities than in villages. And so, in chasing money and careers, people give up their lands along with their proximity to nature. They enter a whole new (urban) world and embrace its grand symbols, its frenetic pace and its plethora of opportunities. From being sons of the soil, they become city slickers. Thus subsequent generations grow up steeped in the urban way of life, the urban way of thinking.

Priyanka started wondering if this mindset of people was actually an opportunity in disguise. Discussing it with her friends, family and faculty mentors, she realized that if, apart from selling plants, she could also offer guidance on maintaining them, her proposition would seem far more attractive to people. Also, she could sell all the tools and implements needed to maintain and nurture plants at home. These would include sprinklers, spades, watering cans, watering hoses, organic manure, insecticides and pesticides, plant shampoo, plant nutrients, etc. These could be used by people who wanted to maintain their plants themselves.

And so, her venture's basket of offerings took shape. She decided to name the company iKheti (to connote personalized farming since 'kheti' means 'farming' in Hindi). She prepared a business plan for iKheti and presented it at Dmagics. The judges felt that given the cramped spaces in Mumbai's houses, iKheti would find it difficult to sell its concept to home dwellers. They felt the company had to find a sound way to tackle this problem.

However, they liked Priyanka's idea for its vision and for the fact that it was addressing an important issue that not many had thought of. They said that with some deeper thinking, the idea could be made to work as a profitable venture.

Priyanka's conviction in the idea certainly helped her sell her concept to the judges. 'Right from the time I hit upon this idea, I was completely convinced that it could be made to work. Not just that, I thought big cities really need more plants, more greenery.'

Mr Raj Bhat, one of the judges on the panel, suggested that if she was really convinced about the idea, she could participate in *The Pitch*, a business reality TV programme that is aired on Bloomberg UTV. Priyanka read up about the programme (check out its Facebook page – www.facebook.com/yourpitch) and found it very exciting. She decided to participate in it. Her next priority was to find an answer to the key question that the judges had posed to her – how would she convince people to set up kitchen gardens in the matchbox-like flats of Mumbai? She knew that this was the make-or-break question for the future of iKheti.

More brainstorming followed. Priyanka realized that changing the mindset of people could take a long time. Entrenched attitudes and biases are very difficult to displace. Also, the average size of each home-farm order was bound to be small. In order to make a sizeable profit, iKheti would have to sell a very large number of plants to homes, which would take a long time and a lot of manpower at one go. The venture might not be very profitable and scalable.

At this stage, she thought she had two options – abandon the idea altogether and take up a job, or keep selling plants to flat-dwellers and be content with the slow progress her venture would make.

But then, a third option occurred to her. Since homes were space-starved, were there other kinds of spaces in Mumbai where she could set up farms? The answer she realized, much to her delight, was yes. She could try taking the concept to corporates and educational institutions.

That sounds odd, right? What place does a farm have in a school, for instance? Will companies have any use for herbs and other edible plants?

But we must look at it this way. More and more schools are keen to impart value-based education to children. Vedic studies, ecology, environment and moral education are a part of the curriculum in many schools across cities. This focus on educating a child holistically means that schools are also keen to bring in novel methods of education such as live demos, a higher degree of practical learning and more field visits.

Having a small farm of edible plants in the campus would therefore make sense to the school management. It would give children direct and close exposure to nature and would build awareness among them about the environment as well as the role it plays in our lives. It would also enhance the greenery in the campuses —which schools are keen on anyway. Very importantly, the edibles grown on the farm can be used by the school canteen.

By having such farms in their campuses, schools would send out a clear message to children about the importance of eating healthy. Priyanka hopes that through the children, she can get this message through to parents, thereby getting them to set up kitchen gardens at home. The same kind of message would hold good for corporate houses too because of the increasing awareness about sustainable living.

Not a bad idea at all, this!

Having decided to add corporate and educational institutions as segments of focus for iKheti, Priyanka reworked the business plan in time for *The Pitch*. Looking back, she feels that participating in *The Pitch* was one of the best things she had done. With its gruelling yet exciting format, it gave her an adrenaline rush as she graduated from one round to the next.

The Pitch also gave her the exposure of a lifetime. She met some of the best CEOs from the corporate world, the best entrepreneurs and the best investors. Not everybody gets a chance to talk to the likes of Ravi Bajaj, Ronnie Screwvala, R. Gopalakrishnan, the Bijli brothers, Neeraj Roy, etc. about their ventures and get feedback from them. 'I found them all to be so humble. It was incredible! And to think that each one of them has had his own share of struggles in life. Their humility and determination are their most outstanding traits,' says Priyanka.

Apart from interacting with industry stalwarts, did she have any other big gain from participating in *The Pitch*? 'Oh, yes! I got in touch with so many interesting people, so many brilliant minds. I learnt the importance of human relationships too.' She struck a rapport with her nine co-contestants, all of whom had interesting business ideas. 'I am in touch with most of them even today.' All the contestants shared a bond with one another, a bond born from the common dream of doing something on their own and making a difference to people. The intense experiences they shared during *The Pitch* have cemented this friendship. 'All of us lead very busy lives, but we manage to keep in touch every once in a while. If I need some help, I know the folks will chip in,' she says.

Chatting with entrepreneurs, industry honchos and investors at *The Pitch* gave Priyanka a wide-angle view of how to approach a business. The leading lights also gave her useful suggestions with regard to her business idea, and by endorsing its potential, reinforced her conviction in her vision.

Throughout her participation in *The Pitch*, iKheti was covered by the media and her business idea got good reviews.

Sometime during *The Pitch*, Priyanka got engaged. Though her fiancé and his parents were comfortably off (they are all chartered accountants), Priyanka made it clear that she did not want to sit idle after getting married. She wanted to do something on her own. Having given birth to the baby called iKheti, there was no way she would abandon it. Thankfully, her fiancé and his parents encouraged her to pursue her entrepreneurial plans.

Happy with her performance at *The Pitch*, and with all that she gained from the contest, Priyanka came back to college on a high. Soon after that came the next high point. Mrs Pratibha Patil, the then president of

India, visited her college to inaugurate the Contributor Development Lab. She told the students that the country needed entrepreneurial thinking in agriculture and urged more students to get into agriculture or agri-business. Priyanka was asked to explain her business idea to the president, who liked it. Priyanka was over the moon! Mrs Patil's words of encouragement boosted her confidence tremendously.

Once college was over, Priyanka formally started operations at iKheti in June 2012. The company has positioned itself as a one-stop shop for urban farms. It offers the following:

- *Consulting*: This essentially involves designing and setting up a kitchen garden from scratch on the customer's premises.
- *Gardening products*: Customers can choose from a wide range including edible plants, organic seeds, customized and designer pots and planters, watering cans/hoses, sprinklers, spades, organic manure, need-based insecticides and pesticides, plant shampoo, etc.
- *Gardener service:* If a customer so wishes, an experienced gardener will visit his/her site at regular intervals to tend to the plants, administer the needed nutrients, medicine, cut/prune the leaves and do everything else a gardener usually does.
- *Workshops on urban farming*: By conducting workshops, Priyanka introduces people to the idea of a kitchen garden and gives them hands-on training on the different kinds of seeds, how to plant them and how

to maintain them. These workshops are a good way of opening up and educating the market, and at the same time promoting iKheti. Once someone has participated in a workshop, the chances are pretty good that he/she will want to buy plants and other products from iKheti. They may even hire Priyanka as a consultant or sign up for the gardener service.

By offering this comprehensive suite of solutions, iKheti comes across as a very professional set-up – several notches higher than the small nurseries and local maalis. I ask her about her team because having the right one is absolutely critical in this specialized field. Priyanka smiles as she says that her maalis form the backbone of her company. She respects them a lot for their earthy wisdom and their instinctive feel for plants. She has learnt a lot about plants by working with them.

As she is telling me this, her phone rings. She answers it and asks the caller to come home in an hour or so. She tells me it is one of her gardeners. He had gone to his native village for a while and has now returned to Mumbai.

Priyanka had felt his absence keenly, what with customers calling her ever so often asking her for a maali. 'My trained maalis are quite popular with my customers.' To people who already have plants at home, but do not know how to maintain them, iKheti's maali service has come as a boon.

Apart from Priyanka herself, iKheti has three maalis, a trained horticulturist, an irrigation specialist and a space designer who ensures optimal utilization of space in installing the farms. Priyanka's husband Sharad Shah takes care of all matters pertaining to finance (which makes sense since he is a CA). Maintaining accounts, measuring returns from the business and talking to investors are things that Sharad handles. Priyanka handles marketing and customer relationships while happily losing herself in the world of plants.

I point out that as she is trying to change entrenched consumer attitudes vis-à-vis plants, it must be difficult to get people to accept what she has to offer. Are her prospective customers usually sceptical when they talk to her, I wonder. She tells me that yes, most people are sceptical about how they can set up a kitchen garden in their premises. 'Is it possible to grow edibles?' is the first question they ask. Next they admit that they don't know much about plants and doubt if they will be able to maintain a kitchen garden on an on-going basis.

To counter this scepticism, Priyanka tries a customized tack in her sales pitch. She visits the prospect's home and checks out the space available. She then talks to the person in detail and understands their aesthetic sensibilities – what kind of a decor do they want? What colours do they like? How have they decorated their premises already? She even finds out if the prospect considers Vaastu important.

With these inputs she comes up with a design solution. Many of iKheti's planters have a very small footprint, that is, they occupy very little floor space. Some planters can even be mounted on the wall or hung on railings. Priyanka is therefore able to place these plants in different parts of the premises. But the clincher is that she has a range of colourful, designer planters that her customers can choose from. That way they get a kitchen garden which looks attractive, one which blends in with and even enhances the decor of the place.

Another thing Priyanka does is ask first-time plant buyers to start slow and easy. She first makes them grow plants like sweet basil, oregano, lemongrass, chillies, curry leaves, etc., which are easy to grow. Once they realize that home-grown edibles are far superior to the ones they get in the market with regard to taste, quality and freshness, she tells them to move a notch higher to vegetables like lettuce, bottle gourd, etc.

This customer-friendly approach has helped iKheti ease into people's homes and hearts. And before they realized it, customers have turned converts. Priyanka recalls many cases of customers falling in love with their kitchen gardens and effusively thanking her for showing them another way of life in such a polluted city.

iKheti's revenues have grown steadily ever since its inception. By and large, Priyanka has chosen the boot-strapping way to grow the venture so far. She did take an interest-free loan from a relative once, when she needed to infuse a large amount of capital into the business. But otherwise she has simply been ploughing back the profits into iKheti.

Now that iKheti has expanded into educational institutions and corporates, the company needs more capital. Setting up farms across bigger areas would mean operations of a considerably larger scale. It will call for greater horticultural expertise. And given that the model is Business to Business (B2B), the payment cycles will be quite long. She will therefore need a larger quantum of working capital at any given point of time. This is why she now wants to bring in a large tranche of money to the business from external sources. iKheti is about to close a deal with an investor to raise the necessary funds and Sharad is helping Priyanka structure the investment deal properly.

Our conversation turns to the topic of finding the right investor for her business. I tell her that she should look for an investor whose wavelength matches hers. Since hers is a specialized and tough business, an investor who belongs to the conventional mould – hankering after a large ROI and seeking a quick exit from the venture – may not fit the bill. Her kind of investor should understand and believe in her vision and should be willing to partner iKheti in its journey ahead. Priyanka nods in thoughtful agreement. She adds that she should be able to trust her investor completely. She believes that trust is probably the most important quality in the investor-investee relationship. Having seen my share of such relationships, I have to agree with her.

'And what about mentors?' I ask. For a venture like hers, aren't they important too?

'Of course!' says Priyanka. 'They have so much more exposure to life and business. They can give us valuable suggestions and put us in touch with the right people.' Mr Kaustubh Dhargalkar, her professor at Welingkar, was a mentor to iKheti in its early days. She gives him credit for supporting her and helping her prepare the blueprint for the company. 'I was a student of the business design course at Welingkar. The course teaches students to approach business with a creative mindset.'

I ask Priyanka about the next steps for iKheti. She tells me that the response from educational institutions has been overwhelming! iKheti has now started discussing the concept of urban farms with corporate houses and builders too and is also close to setting up farms in a few corporate premises.

Now that her business has stabilized in the residential segment and has entered other sectors, Priyanka is keen to formally get trained in horticulture. She knows that formal training will vastly enhance her knowledge and smooth out the rough edges. She will then be able to give her sales pitch that extra edge and supervise the work of her team better.

In late 2014, iKheti opened its first retail store in Bandra, Mumbai. An entire range of potted plants and implements is available at the store. Having this store helps because people definitely like to touch and see plants before they buy them. The company plans to open more stores in a phased manner.

In tune with the times, iKheti has started selling products on its website and other social media sites as well. People living in Mumbai and Pune can have these products home delivered too. Priyanka wants to start offering door step delivery to other cities soon. This move will expand her market manifold at a disproportionately low cost.

Importing plants and gardening products is another item on her 'to-do' list. The products available in some countries in the West are very robust and thoughtfully designed.

Interesting and ambitious plans, all of them. Priyanka however wants to make them happen one at a time. She's careful not to bite off more than she can chew. She'd rather do only one thing at a time, but do it extremely well.

Changing the mindset of people is going to be a long-drawn task. The iKheti team knows that there will be moments of despair along the way. In spite of all that, Priyanka is confident that her team will continue to scale the challenges they encounter along the way.

Today, iKheti is a profitable and growing enterprise. As it keeps spreading its roots and sprouting green shoots, here's wishing it all the best for the future!

SIDELIGHTS

- Priyanka spends most of her free time with her cats – she has eight of them! As a child, she used to go looking for stray kittens and bring them home. 'A pet on your lap and a plant on your windowsill are all you need to be happy' is her credo in life.
- On one of her birthdays, she asked her friends to not gift her anything, but instead asked that they donate some

money to an animal care organization to help treat a dog. She raised Rs 10,000 and the dog was successfully treated. Her friends said that, but for her urging, the thought would never have occurred to them.

Priyanka's Message to Young Entrepreneurs

- It is important to either have total conviction in one's idea or be convinced that one can't set up a venture. It is also important to try and understand one's expectations from life. If you have started something and are convinced about its potential, then pursue it no matter what.
- As Victor Hugo famously said, 'All the forces in the world are not so powerful as an idea whose time has come.'

Key Learnings from Priyanka's Story

- There can be profitable business opportunities in the areas of ecology/environment and sustainable living.
- An idea from the past can be resurrected and taken to the market even today. The important thing is to repackage it according to current market tastes, realities and challenges. Priyanka has simply repackaged the old concept of kitchen gardens to suit the cramped apartments of today, adding a touch of glamour to them!
- If there is someone in the family whose skills will be useful to your venture, consider taking that person

on board. He/she can be of help, at least in the initial stages of the venture.
- When you are trying to change an entrenched mindset in people, you have to be very patient. You will definitely get results if you keep chipping away.

5. Tech Innovance Pune

Founders: Prasad Gundecha and Akshat Oswal
Name of the company: Tech Innovance
Brand name: Tech Innovance
Nature of business: Home and building automation; automated security solutions.
Founded in: 2012
Based in: Pune
Team size: Five
Vision for the business: To provide solutions that enhance people's lifestyle in a sustainable, energy-efficient manner.
URL: www.techinnovance.com

This is an industry that calls for a high degree of technical expertise, access to reputed vendors and a wide range of products in your portfolio. Worldwide and in India, it is a mature industry that sees frequent advancements in technology. So you need to be on your toes all the time. You have to constantly keep track of technological trends, ensure you have the latest products in your kitty and know how to install, commission and repair them. But more than anything else, you need guts. Guts to take on big daddies like Siemens, L&T and ABB.

We are talking about the building automation and security systems industry.

This is the story of how Akshat Oswal and Prasad Gundecha are carving a niche for themselves in this tough business through their company Tech Innovance Pvt. Ltd.

A One-Touch Life

Oddly enough, Akshat and Prasad are in this high-tech business today thanks to the humble khakhra, a traditional papad-like snack which is routinely made and eaten in thousands of Gujarati households. To understand how this happened, let's go back to the days when the two of them were studying business management at Sadhana Centre for Management and Leadership Development in Pune.

Akshat recalls the exhilaration of being in college. Their daily schedule was gruelling, not unlike that of a military training programme. At the same time though, it was exciting. Each day would begin at 6.30 a.m. with yoga and meditation. After that, classes would begin and go on till 8.30 in the evening. After a quick dinner the students would re-group to finish their assignments and prepare for the next day's classes. It was a routine that any student of a management institute would instantly relate to.

As part of the curriculum, all students had to participate in an activity called 'Out of the Box'. As the name suggests, the activity was created to make students think differently. It was held every alternate Thursday and mandated that every student had to sell something and make at least Rs 300 per head. As it happened, Prasad and Akshat joined hands and decided to sell snacks, something Indians love to dig in to.

One Thursday, they set up a stall at Kamala Nehru Park in Pune and sold bhel, khakhras and sandwiches. They sourced the khakhras from Akshat's aunt, who used to make them at home and sell them to people in her neighbourhood. When they counted their profits at the end of the day, they were very surprised! They had made a profit of a cool Rs 1000 in a single day. The classmates cum partners calculated that, at this rate, they could earn Rs 30,000 per month by merely selling street food at a single stall!

They put up the stall at the same place for the next few Thursdays and earned decent sums of money each time. Akshat and Prasad realized that, by selling street food, they too had become entrepreneurs.

'We did not know each other very well at that time. But selling khakhras and bhel together made us get to know each other better. We became friends.'

Both of them are eternally grateful to their college for including the 'Out of the Box' activity in the curriculum of management studies and making every student participate. Come to think of it, conducting the activity was out of the box thinking on the part of the college management!

I realize that this activity was solely responsible for making entrepreneurs out of Akshat and Prasad. It changed their way of thinking and convinced them that they could run a business on their own. In short, it changed their lives.

Like all good entrepreneurs, they did not want to let matters rest there. The big question on their minds was, 'How do we make use of this experience?' They were both equally keen to build on what they had learnt over the past few Thursdays. Logic told them that they should try selling the same kind of edibles over a longer time frame and see what happens. Akshat's aunt (who supplied them with khakhras) was facing financial troubles. The two friends thought they could ask her to make khakhras, sell them through kirana and snack food stores, and then give her the lion's share of the earnings. This way they would help her tide over her financial troubles and at the same time make some money themselves.

The two youngsters spoke to a few shopkeepers and convinced them to stock their home-made khakhras. They would get the khakhras from Akshat's aunt and take them to Prasad's house. There, in a room which Prasad's parents had allowed them to use for their business, they would sort and pack the khakhras, stick a label on each pack and then send out the supplies to retailers. They sold the khakhras under the brand name 'Reet'. Soon they started selling them in a few different flavours. The delicious khakhras were a hit in the market. Though they were available at only a few stores, they soon acquired a loyal set of customers who kept coming back for more. The retailers were only too happy to stock these khakhras.

Profitability was decent; the snacks fetched the two friends a good bit of money. As planned earlier, they gave Akshat's aunt her share.

Life went on like that for some time. Prasad and Akshat had their hands full with their internship, studies and their cottage industry-scale business. Somewhere at the back of their minds though, was the question, 'Should we be doing something more? Something else?'

One day Akshat's cousin, who is a distributor of a range of electrical products to companies, told him that the building automation business was good and growing fast. He asked Akshat to seriously consider entering this business, possibly as a supplier of products or as a consultant. Akshat was surprised at first, caught off-guard. He knew nothing about building automation. He hadn't even known until then that it was a full-fledged industry. To add to that, he had no prior connection to or experience in home automation. True, he did have a graduate degree in computer science. However, he wasn't sure if such a degree had equipped him to work with automation systems.

In any case, he decided to read up on the industry and its prospects. To his surprise, he found that it was a well established and very profitable across the world. Even in India, automation of commercial and corporate buildings had become a big thing since the turn of the millennium. With the increasing construction of malls, IT parks, large corporate zones and SEZs, the demand for automation and security solutions for buildings had shot up many times over.

Indian homes, on the other hand, painted a different picture altogether. In this segment, automation is largely unheard of. Barring a miniscule number of homes belonging to the ultra-rich, most homes in India run on manual controls. Think about it – how many houses have you seen with automated garage doors, lighting controls or appliance controls?

When Akshat read up about the industry and spoke to a few people who knew how it worked, he got the feeling that maybe with a considerable amount of effort, he and Prasad could pull it off. They would set up shop as consultants in home automation and security and test the waters for a while. If things went well, they would continue. Akshat's cousin Mr Pritam Oswal, who is a distributor of ABB products in Pune, encouraged Akshat to go for it.

Akshat discussed the idea with Prasad. At first, Prasad wanted to take up a job. But then he thought back to the days when he sold khakhras and bhel and realized that he had had loads of fun while earning some money at the same time. That was also the time when he had struck up a great personal and professional rapport with Akshat. He knew that the two of them made a good team. He gave the matter a lot of thought, Akshat seemed very keen on going into business with him.

So perhaps he *should* give it a try. He decided to join Akshat in taking the plunge and told him that he would try out this business wholeheartedly for a year. If their company did not reach a certain size and stabilize in one year, he would pull out, to which Akshat agreed. And they were in business!

The duo's thinking was like this – they knew that the industry had scope for growth and was profitable. If they could start by focusing on the residential segment and stabilize in it over a period of time, they could carve out a niche for themselves. After that they could decide to what extent they could expand the business within the same segment. They could decide whether or not they wanted to enter the high stakes, high competition 'commercial buildings' segment. They knew instinctively that attacking the 'commercial buildings' segment right in the beginning would be the wrong thing to do.

It sounded like a plan!

Of course, in order to get started, they would need to get trained in automation platforms, software and products. Akshat's cousin had a useful suggestion. He told them about KNX, a German multinational that makes software for building automation systems. KNX is widely known in the industry and has a fierce reputation for being right at the top as an automation platform. Essentially, KNX provided a software platform with which automation and security products manufactured by more than 350 companies across the world were compatible. This means that if you are a KNX Certified Partner (which you become after getting trained on their platform), you could choose from a list of 350 top-notch brands and offer them to your customer.

To Akshat and Prasad, KNX sounded like the right brand to go with. With the stamp of 'KNX Certified

Partner', they knew they would gain credibility in the eyes of prospective customers. Selling their services would be that much easier.

In October 2012, both of them attended a five-day training programme on KNX in Bengaluru. After returning to Pune, they finalized the role each one would play in the new venture. That was a rather easy decision to take as both of them knew what the other was good at. Akshat's strengths, they knew, lay in networking with people, nurturing relationships and selling. Giving him the mandate of business development and marketing was therefore a logical decision. Prasad, on the other hand, was the more technically-minded of the two, being at ease with the software and hardware they had to deal with. Also, he was good with vendors. Therefore, his role was to come up with customized solutions for their clientele, identify the right vendors and handle relations with them.

They decided to name the company Tech Innovance, alluding to the high-tech nature of their business and the need to keep innovating in order to stay ahead of others in the field.

Their first order was very small. Someone wanted a security camera installed in his house. Akshat found a camera vendor through Justdial, the online directory service, and gave him the task of installing a camera at the client's house. 'We were complete novices then. We didn't even know how a security camera worked. We learnt by observing the camera vendor,' laughs Prasad.

Adds Akshat, 'Yeah, right. We have learnt a lot from our vendors and electrical contractors every step of the way. It has been an eye-opening experience for us.'

But that first order gave the partners a minor shock because they incurred a loss of Rs 300 on it. They realized they were paying more to the camera vendor than what they were making from their client. In other words, they had under-quoted. However, the loss did not bother them much. They earned the trust and respect of their first client and got to know a few vendors in the market. They knew that their monetary loss could be recouped very soon. That said, they have been extra careful in quoting prices ever since.

Soon after that, Akshat and Prasad got another lead. This one involved automating five row houses in Baner, an area that had come into prominence over the last few years. The lead came to them from Akshat's cousin, but Akshat was not confident about bagging this order. Theirs was a two-man fledgling set-up. Even if they got the order, would they be able to execute it? This project involved a certain level of complexity and scale. In any case, he decided to meet the prospective customer, the builder who was constructing the five row houses, and see how it would go. He found out that a larger competitor was also pitching for this order and that it had already met the builder.

However, this competitor had tried to dazzle the client with a lot of technical jargon in its sales presentation. Also, the solution it had recommended did not meet the builder's design of the row houses.

Akshat sensed that Tech Innovance had half a chance to bag this order. He knew what to do. He met the builder and spoke to him about home automation in layman's terms. Using simple terms, he explained to him the principles of home automation and how it could make life easy for those who would occupy the houses. In other words, he relegated the technical aspects of the automation system to the background and highlighted the benefits of using the system.

The builder was impressed with Akshat's presentation and gave the order to Tech Innovance. They negotiated a little on the value of the order and finally reached an agreement. Akshat and Prasad were over the moon! Tech Innovance had bagged an order worth Rs 18 lakh! Since they were operating on a decent profit margin, bagging this order meant that their business would have a small pile of extra cash.

Akshat and Prasad's families were happy with their progress. Akshat's cousin kept giving them suggestions and putting them in touch with the right people. 'He has been a big source of help and encouragement,' says Prasad. 'In fact, he was the one who pointed out that we were plugging a key gap in the market by providing home automation solutions.' Another major source of help and guidance has been Ashay Shah, the founder of Furute, an organization that provides training in leadership and development of people. The training that Akshat and Prasad underwent at Furute helped them design proper systems and procedures at Tech Innovance. Also, it helped them comb the market scientifically and thereby acquire more customers.

Here is a short note on home automation for those who came in late. The broad objective of automating a house is to help people calibrate and control their gadgets and appliances the way they want, keeping their preferences and conveniences in mind. Home automation gives you enormous flexibility in remote operating everything at home. From your air-conditioner to the lights, fans and even window blinds. For instance, while sitting on your couch, you can dim the lights in your living room by merely pressing a button on a remote control console. From the same couch, you could switch on the AC in your bedroom so that the room is cool by the time you actually want to turn in.

Further, you can set the mood of the room according to your wish. Imagine the curtains of your room opening automatically at 7 a.m. and liquid notes of music washing over you. On your way home after a harried day at work, you could switch on the AC in your living room from your car using your Android phone or iPad. By the time you reach home, the room has cooled to just the right temperature! Similarly, if you forgot to turn off the clothes iron or the geyser when you left home, you could switch it off through your phone or iPad. You get the drift – the possibilities are many!

A home automation system gives new meaning to the word 'convenience'. It presents to you things you never imagined existed.

Typically, when your home is automated, you can control the mechanism in three different ways. One is through the automation switches, which look like regular electrical switches. The second (and most preferred) mode is through a remote control panel. The third is through your smartphone or a device like an iPad. Since smartphones and iPads are being used by an increasingly large number of people, more users of home automation would start operating the controls through such devices in the future.

A wide range of home automation systems is available in the market. You can choose the kind you want to deploy at home depending on the level of sophistication you are looking for. Which is directly linked to the money you are willing to spend on it.

Since home automation is a nascent industry in India, companies operating in this space have to work extra hard to make consumers understand what they are offering. This is concept selling in its truest form. The trick therefore, is to first understand the kind of flexibility and control a potential customer wants and then his budget for automation/security. With this information, Tech Innovance comes up with a solution and presents it to the potential consumer. Explaining the solution and its benefits in very simple language can make all the difference. As Akshat says, 'The point is to make the prospective customer see the kind of lifestyle he can lead after implementing this system. At the same time, we should not try to impress him with technical terms or show him too many product options. That will only confuse him.'

The partners learnt this fundamental truth the hard way. For the first three months after starting up, they used to throw a lot of technical content at potential customers. When they failed to convert a number of enquiries, they started wondering if something was wrong with their sales pitch. This was when they realized that customers expected to hear and see what an automation system can *do* for them rather than hear too much about its components or technicalities.

The benefit-oriented sales approach has worked very well for Tech Innovance. As of now, they have successfully executed more than fifty orders in home automation and security solutions. A while ago, they picked up the order for automating the house of the owner of a five-star hotel in Pune. This person is widely known in Pune's business and social circles. Akshat and Prasad knew that if they executed this order well, it would be a big step forward for their company. They could use this order to bag other orders in the future.

In a major step forward, Tech Innovance set up an 'experience centre' in May 2014. The centre is meant to give people a live experience of how different products work and demonstrate their full potential. Akshat and Prasad bring prospective customers, architects, interior designers and electrical contractors to this experience centre for live demos. All of them go back impressed.

Already there are signs that setting up the 'experience centre' has been a game changer for them. The turnover of the company has doubled since the time it opened this centre and the customer base has increased considerably.

The company is now ready to scout for business from other parts of Maharashtra.

In another forward-thinking move, the company recently set up an R&D team. While it is currently a small unit, the idea is to keep testing different products and see if, in the long run, innovative products in building automation can be developed in-house.

Today, Tech Innovance has a team of eight highly competent professionals, including the founders. Prabhat Sachan, Piyush, Amol and Vinayak are a few other key members of their team.

From hawking bhel and khakhras to becoming consultants in home automation and security, Akshat and Prasad's lives have transformed beyond belief. The youngsters entered a nascent industry and learnt the ropes the hard way. Today, they are changing the lifestyle of their customers. They have not only acquired a reputation for being highly professional, but have also built a profitable business for themselves.

And now they are all set to soar!

Sidelights

- Both Prasad and Akshat want to open a restaurant sometime in the future. They do not know when they will do it, only that they *will*.
- Akshat goes cycling every morning and covers at least 4 km. Prasad is an amateur disc jockey. He enjoys DJ'ing for small groups of friends.

Prasad and Akshat's Message to Young Entrepreneurs

- When you set out to do something on your own, give yourself a time limit. Tell yourself that you will give your best to the new venture for a certain period of time and then take stock of the progress you have achieved. During this time frame, you have to be completely focused on the venture to make it work. There is no set formula for calculating this time limit. It just depends on the industry you are going to operate in and your personal comfort level.
- If you believe in an idea, give it your all. The results will follow automatically. Just focus on making the idea work.
- Do not be put off by failures. They are the pillars on which success is built.

Key Learnings from Prasad and Akshat's Story

- Do not be scared of entering an industry that is high-tech and which already has a number of big players. Through smart play you can still grab a share of the pie. The trick is to start small and then keep improving and growing. Try to identify a niche and focus on it.
- When you enter a high-tech industry for which you don't have all the necessary knowledge, get trained immediately.

- When trying to acquire business, speak in a language the prospective customer understands. Clearly bring out the benefits of buying the product or service you are offering. The trick is to make them see how you are satisfying their need.
- Try to think unconventionally and be a step ahead of other companies in your industry, especially if you are a small player. Akshat and Prasad have opened the Experience Centre, which most companies in this industry in India have not done. This is proving to be a game changer for Tech Innovance!

6. Biosyl Technologies Hubli

Founders: Sarah D'Souza and Amit Vernekar
Name of the company: Biosyl Technologies Private Limited
Brand name: Anaerobio
Nature of business: Design, production and installation of cost-effective anaerobic chambers for the growth and analysis of anaerobic bacteria cultures.
Founded in: 2012
Based in: Hubli
Team size: Three
Vision for the business: To come up with innovative ideas and creative solutions in biotechnology.
URL: www.facebook.com/biosyl

Nearly all the students who graduate from the Hubli – Dharwad belt move to Bengaluru in search of jobs. By staying back in Hubli and becoming entrepreneurs, Sarah D'Souza and Amit Vernekar are doing something drastically different from the norm. And they are happy about it.

I can see why life in a small city like Hubli has many attractions. Being a laid-back place, the pace of life here is languid. People are able to finish work and still find time to do other things every day. More importantly, for a start-up, the cost of doing business here is much lower than in a big city. Office and house rentals are lower and it is easier to find competent people at lower salaries.

Already a small but growing tribe of start-ups have recognized these realities and set up base in Hubli.

Sarah and Amit have overcome a number of hurdles to set up Biosyl. This is the fascinating story of their resourcefulness and persistence.

Culture Matters

Sarah D'Souza and Amit Vernekar met as classmates at B.V. Bhoomaraddi College of Engineering and Technology, Hubli (BVB College). Both of them joined the Engineering course in 2008.

The story of Biosyl started in 2011, when both of them were in their final year at college. The students had to do a project on a topic of their choice. Sarah and Amit were keen to do theirs on anaerobic bacteria because of their interest in the topic. Also, they found that most people chose to do projects or conduct research on aerobic bacteria. Sarah and Amit were keen to do something different.

A brief note on aerobic and anaerobic bacteria. Aerobic bacteria need oxygen to live and grow while anaerobic bacteria survive only in the *absence* of oxygen. Identifying whether a bacterium is an aerobe or anaerobe is important in many ways, especially in the treatment of bacterial infections.

Unfortunately, Sarah and Amit found that their college did not have an anaerobic culturing system (which is necessary to cultivate and grow bacteria under anaerobic conditions) to carry out their project. Disappointed, they had to settle for a project on aerobic culturing studies.

However, the itch to carry out studies in anaerobic bacteria remained. 'We used to keep jotting down ideas in our notebooks on how to build an efficient anaerobic system. We also used to read up a lot about the subject and speak to our professors about it.'

Finally one day, they decided to experiment with a particular idea. They made a glass cube and created a vacuum inside it. To check if the chamber was indeed a vacuum, they placed a lit candle inside it. After a while the candle got extinguished automatically, leading them to the assumption that it had used up all the remnant oxygen in the cube. They were thus left with an anaerobic chamber.

'We showed the cube to our professor, Ms Swati Hegde (who teaches bio-instrumentation and bio-sensors in our college). She encouraged us to improvise and build further on the idea,' says Amit animatedly.

While this idea had been attempted by a few other people earlier, Sarah and Amit's design brought down the cost of constructing the anaerobic chamber. Moving forward, there was a good chance that their design would use resources more efficiently than the other designs available in the market.

From interactions with their professors and industry experts, they had come to know that culturing of anaerobic bacteria was being done predominantly using crude equipment, like jars. The equipment was inefficient and suffered from quite a few problems. Chief among the problems was the fact that they could not guarantee the total absence of oxygen which is vital for anaerobic studies. Sarah and Amit thought that colleges would need a more sophisticated, more efficient method of culturing anaerobic bacteria. At the same time however, any new method would have to be cost effective too in order to find wide acceptance. The more they talked about it, the more they felt that the glass anaerobic chamber they had built was a good start. With some refinements, it could be sold to labs in colleges

And so, they decided to make a bigger working model of the same chamber in time for the National Tech Fest the next year. This was an event their college conducted every year. They wanted this model to be more efficient and robust than the miniature they had made earlier.

Unfortunately, they did not have any idea how to go about it. Several questions plagued them – what materials to use? How much would these materials cost? What technical specifications should they adhere to?

They studied a number of materials that could possibly be used to construct the cube. They also had long and intense conversations with their professors on the subject.

Finally, they decided to use glass for the chamber in their prototype. It took them a month to construct and assemble it. The dimensions of the glass cube they had built were 1.5 x 2 x 1.5 feet.

To test the absence of oxygen inside the cube, they placed a sample of Clostridium, a genus of anaerobic bacteria, inside the cube. The bacteria grew, proving that they had succeeded. If there had been even a trace of oxygen, the bacteria would not have grown.

Amit and Sarah eagerly presented this prototype at the National Tech Fest in 2011. Though the two classmates had put in their best efforts and had burned the midnight oil, they did not know how their model would fare at the event. Would the judges like it? Would they think it was good enough to commercialize? Or would it be seen as an amateurish effort? They were anxious to find out.

Surprise, surprise! Their entry won the third prize. The judges were impressed with their product and said that there was definitely a need for it in the market. At the same time, they asked Sarah and Amit to fine-tune it more. For instance, they pointed out that glass could burst at high pressure so maybe they should use steel. Also, since the chamber was divided into two compartments, they suggested improvising on the locking system between the two compartments and introducing some add-ons to the system to improve functionality.

Sarah and Amit set to work on these valuable suggestions. Using mild steel instead of glass for the body made the chamber safer while keeping the cost low. In order to conserve the resources used, like gas and power, the duo introduced a chamber, thereby dividing the existing chamber into two – a bigger part and a smaller part. Throughout this period, one of their professors, Swati Hedge, was a source of great help and comfort to the youngsters. 'We used to trouble her a lot; go to her with all sorts of questions and doubts,' grins Sarah. The professor's help was invaluable to the duo; if it weren't for her help, they would have taken much longer to build a good product.

They presented this model at another state-level tech fest conducted in Mangalore a short while later. While all the judges liked their work, one of them was particularly impressed. This gentleman worked with Jubilant Biosys, a company based in Bengaluru. He told the youngsters that they should not underestimate the commercial potential of their product. He asked them to start selling it soon.

Here was an industry expert praising the work of two students, youngsters from an unknown college in a small town. No wonder Sarah and Amit found his words tremendously encouraging. What's more, the judges awarded the duo a 'special appreciation' prize for their product.

Over the next couple of months, Sarah and Amit had endless conversations on how to take this product to the market. By now, thanks to the sustained positive feedback they had received, they were sure their product was a winner.

However, to make their creation a success, they would have to turn entrepreneurs as soon as they graduated from college. This would mean giving up a safe and steady path (of being employed in a good firm) for the turbulent path of entrepreneurship. Were they prepared for that? This question haunted them for weeks on end as they were wary of the risk involved. Also, they did not know how to convince their parents. Sarah and Amit were thoroughly confused!

At the time of graduating, they came to know that a few of their classmates had joined hands to set up a company in the field of e-learning. After speaking to them, Sarah and Amit learnt that their college was providing basic support to their venture by giving them space to set up an office and a laboratory. Surprised and emboldened by this discovery, Sarah and Amit decided that they too would approach the college for help. If the college agreed, it would be a big step in the pursuit of their dreams.

But first, they spoke to their parents about their desires and, with great difficulty, managed to have their way.

Next, they met the vice principal of their college, who agreed to support them on the condition that they convince him of the market potential of this product. He asked them to conduct a survey of the intended consumer segments and present a report to him. Grabbing this chance, Sarah and Amit got cracking. Over the next month, they systematically assessed the need for their product. They spoke to representatives of laboratories, research institutions, educational institutions and pharmaceutical companies. The professors of their college helped them design the survey and meet the right respondents.

The results of the market study surprised them. A good percentage of the people they met agreed that their product addressed a strong need. Many of them were looking for a cost-effective chamber for studying anaerobic cultures, but could not find good anaerobic workstations in the market. Moreover, the survey threw up possibilities they had not thought of. For instance, when they had started the survey, they had been under the impression that their product could only be sold to labs in educational institutions. Speaking to the respondents however, they found that pharmaceutical companies and research establishments could also be targeted.

When the vice principal read their report, he immediately sent them to Professor Nitin Kulkarni, the head of Centre for Technology and Entrepreneurship (CTE), a start-up incubator. CTE is a part of BVB College itself and has its office and incubation centre inside the college campus. Nitin liked their business idea. He noticed that though Sarah and Amit did not know anything about the business, they were hard-working and eager to take their idea to its logical conclusion. He gladly agreed to extend all possible help to them. This included giving them office space and access to the labs at CTE. 'By giving us these facilities free of cost, Nitin helped our venture get a solid start. Getting to work from here instead of having to find an office in town and paying rent for it has helped us a lot. Also, it is impossible to find such good labs elsewhere in Hubli!' says Amit.

Sarah and Amit decided to name their company 'Biosyl Technologies' ('bio' referring to life sciences and 'syl' meaning connect). They wanted the name to connote the fact that they are connecting technology to life.

On 14 July 2012, the entrepreneurs started working from their office at the incubation centre. 'Having our own office was an unbelievable feeling!' Sarah tells me, unable to hold back her grin.

But the real grind began only now.

They learnt AutoCAD and created a rough design of the anaerobic chamber they had conceived. An AutoCAD professional in Hubli helped them fine-tune and finish their design. The next step was to fabricate a model based on it. This proved to be tougher than they thought. The reason was simple – Sarah and Amit wanted their product to adhere to FDA standards because they are the best in the world. However, not many people in this field in India are conversant with these standards. Finding a good fabricator who would not just adhere to the standards, but also give the product a good finish proved to be a real struggle. Finally, after searching far and wide, they got their product built by someone who fabricates baking equipment in Bengaluru.

Sarah and Amit brought the model back to Hubli. Since they could not find anyone to assemble the circuitry and give the model the final touches, they ended up doing it themselves.

And finally, in January 2013, the prototype was ready! Understandably, the two entrepreneurs heaved a sigh of relief. This was an important milestone for them.

Their joy doubled when they heard that they had made it to the final round of the Tata First Dot competition for student entrepreneurs. Ms Vanishree Acharya, a mentor of theirs, had suggested that they participate in this competition. The final round was held at IIT Madras in January 2013. For the novelty of their product and for trying to build a business venture around it, Sarah and Amit won the Jury's Choice Award as India's top student start-up.

This competition was immensely useful to them. They got their idea and venture evaluated by the top investors and entrepreneurs of India, they met a lot of bright minds, did extensive networking and were covered by the media too. 'Most people we met were surprised that we were building a venture based in Hubli!'

In March 2013, Shristee (a classmate in college) joined Biosyl after a short stint at Biocon, Bengaluru. She was excited by the idea of working in a start-up and doing something original rather than working in a corporate set-up. Two years down the line, she is extremely happy that she took that step. 'In a start-up, you get to contribute much more than you can in a big company. You also learn so much more. The three of us work as equals here,' says Shristee.

Biosyl has segmented the market into three:
1. Alpha – Educational institutions which need only basic models of their product.
2. Beta – Research institutes and Micro, Small and Medium Enterprises(MSMEs) which require a more complex, more precise version.
3. Gamma – Large companies and factories. These include manufacturers of ethanol, pharmaceutical

companies and companies involved in hypoxy tissue culture.

For some time, Biosyl will cater only to the Alpha and Beta segments. Sarah explains the logic behind this decision. 'Our main objective is to offer affordable yet effective systems for growing anaerobic cultures. There is a big unaddressed need in educational institutions and small companies. This is what we want to plug first.'

With the Alpha model ready for sale, Biosyl has been approaching potential customers, pitching the product to them and sending them proposals. Meanwhile, they have approached the University for Agricultural Sciences, Dharwad for a technical recommendation of their product. This, they believe, will help their product find more acceptance in the market.

The team is also working on developing some consumables. Shristee tells me that since the anaerobic workstation/chamber is a one-time buy for customers, they want to develop and sell consumables too. This would ensure a more steady inflow of revenue.

I note that Sarah and Amit have taken a little longer than expected in hitting the market. This is mainly because of two reasons. First, they had to grope around in the darkness for the first few months since they did not have a clue about how to get started on their venture. Second, they wanted to be sure that their product was indeed robust and adhered to the highest quality standards.

They feel that the extra time they have spent in preparing the ground for Biosyl and in fine-tuning their product will help them. Amit says, 'Now that we are thoroughly prepared, we are confident that our product will be a success. We are making a good first impression on the people we meet. Also, we won't have to keep on fixing bugs in our product.'

Sarah and Amit have reason to feel happy. For being smart enough to spot a latent need in the market and developing a solution for it. For venturing into an unusual business domain. For setting high standards for themselves and trying to build a good product, even if they had to struggle to do so. And finally, for going against the grain and setting up their venture in a small town.

Sidelights

- Sarah is a passionate nail artist and an avid reader.
- Amit finds interior design fascinating and constantly occupies himself with interior design projects. He's also interested in numismatics and cooking.

Sarah and Amit's Message to Young Entrepreneurs

- Follow your dreams or you will spend the rest of your days working for someone who did.
- Be passionate, think big and stay committed. Just sit back and enjoy the bumpy ride. As Milton Berle said, 'If opportunity doesn't knock, build a door.'

Key Learnings from Amit and Sarah's Story

- Consider setting up your venture in a small town, especially one that has reasonably good infrastructure and is well connected to a big city. That way you will keep your operating costs lower without having to live in Timbuktu. The Internet will help you keep in touch with your vendors, customers, investors and other associates who may be living elsewhere.
- Do your homework and get your product right *before* hitting the market. At the same time, do not spend too much time doing so. The trick is to bring the product to an acceptable standard as soon as possible and then start selling it. In Biosyl's case, they could have started selling the initial versions of the product in the eighth month or so, instead of waiting for a full year. At the same time, they could have continued fine-tuning it at the back end. Remember, the sooner you start clocking sales, the better.

7. iGenero
Hyderabad

Founders: Aditya Gupta, Armin Baig and Karan Kumar
Name of the company: iGenero Web Solutions Pvt. Ltd
Brand name: iGenero
Nature of business: Web and mobile technology services, branding and communication design services, digital marketing.
Founded in: 2008
Based in: Hyderabad
Team size: Nine
Vision for the business: To accentuate brand messages through a streamlined communication and design strategy with a strong technical backbone.
URL: www.igenero.com

Avid bikers Aditya Gupta and Armin Baig along with movie buff Karan S. Kumar got together in 2008 to set up iGenero. With no corporate experience worth the mention, they entered an industry that was already crowded. Unfazed by the existing competition, the trio set out to find their identity in the online space. What started as a three-man outfit that designed basic websites has now become a company which is sought after for its solutions in design, development and branding for both web and mobile media.

iGenero has managed to build long-term relationships with its clients and foster a great work culture while growing constantly over the past five years. At the same time however, they have had their share of struggles.

The young promoters know that they still have a long way to go. But with age on their side and oodles of guts and confidence, they know they will go far. Read on to know all about them.

The Digital Musketeers

We meet at a coffee shop on Church Street in Bengaluru's original fashion district. It is a Sunday morning. The sky is overcast and the weather is cool. The monsoon rains have set in. As I enter the coffee shop, I find Aditya already seated at a table. Though based in Hyderabad, he has come to Bengaluru to attend a networking event organized by his other start-up venture, Social Samosa. Aditya tells me that the attendance at the event was overwhelming. 'We were expecting about 100 people, but nearly 250 turned up!' He managed to get a lot of business leads for Social Samosa and iGenero. Though it is a Sunday, his email inbox is being bombarded by prospective clients he met at the event. Aditya is understandably happy.

He orders a mint lemon tea while I ask for some masala chai. I ask him how iGenero came into being and he starts narrating the story of his entrepreneurial journey. I sit back and listen closely.

Most people study engineering in the hope that they will get a good job later. Aditya decided to study engineering out of curiosity. 'People were talking about it so much. I wanted to see what it was all about,' he says with a grin.

While studying engineering, he was clear that he would pursue his master's degree abroad. So he did not even attend the on-campus placement interviews.

In his final year of engineering, Aditya, like most others in his batch, applied to many universities in the USA for admission to their master's programme. He not only got admission but even won scholarships from a couple of them. However, at the last minute, he decided that it would be better to first get some work experience in India before studying further. He thought it would give him a practical knowledge of how things work in companies. That would come in handy later on. He therefore decided to defer his plans to study further and pursue higher studies the next year, if things went well.

After graduating he joined a company called Azri Solutions in Hyderabad. By doing so, he went against the prevalent norm. In Andhra Pradesh, most engineering graduates are hell-bent on doing one of two things – enrol in a master's programme abroad or start working in big, well-known IT companies immediately. The whole focus is to win a scholarship or get a job with a high salary. In other words, opt for the financial security that comes with having a set career path.

Aditya chose to do neither of these.

Azri was a hard-core IT company, specializing in high-end web-based projects for companies. Most of its clients were from the USA and Europe. His stint in Azri introduced him to the fascinating world of the Internet. That was the time when Internet 2.0 had just become the next big thing. Facebook and Orkut had just entered people's lives and were quite the rage. His job was to read up about random topics on the web – for instance, on how the industry was shaping up, what the emerging trends were, etc. At times, he was even asked by his seniors to work out the nitty-gritty of certain projects on the basis of information available on the web. All this meant that Aditya got to spend a lot of time on the Internet every day.

And he was hooked!

He loved the time he spent at Azri. Long hours in front of the computer opened up his mind to the tremendous business possibilities that were emerging through the Internet. Plus, Azri was a chilled-out start-up. It did not believe in binding its employees to strict rules. The atmosphere in office was very informal. Employees came and went whenever they wanted as long as they finished their work on time. 'My interview with the top guy at Azri actually took place over a smoke, can you believe it?' Aditya throws his head back and laughs.

His salary at that time was about Rs 12,000 or 13,000. He thought that for a first job it was par for the course. More than anything else, he loved the work culture of the company and the learning opportunities it gave him.

Six months into the job at Azri, he asked for a salary hike. He did get a raise, but it was less than what he wanted. Aditya was not happy, but at the same time he was not sure about his next step. Around then the entrepreneurial bug bit him. He had been toying with the idea of starting a business of his own. In fact, for a long time his father had been urging him to set up his own business. Any business of his choice. His family members have been businessmen for generations.

'I thought maybe this was the right time to try setting up my own venture,' reminisces Aditya. He thought that since he was still very young, he would try running his business for some time and see if things worked out. If not, he could explore other avenues later. And so, he quit Azri. But the question remained – what business should he go into? He had no clear answers.

He discussed this issue with a couple of friends, Karan and Armin (both of whom had been his college mates). The three of them were on the same wavelength and of similar temperament. While they did not know each other very well then, they did like one another. Karan and Armin were having some problems with their current jobs so they too were wondering what their next steps should be.

They decided to try setting up a business together. After several rounds of brainstorming, they came up with three ideas for their venture.

One idea was to do something in the domain of Internet-based solutions. They knew it was already crowded with several companies, but that also probably meant there was money in that domain.

The second option was to manufacture high quality bike-riding gear. Armin and Aditya were proud owners of Enfield Bullet motorcycles and knew that good quality riding gear was not widely/easily available in India. What was available were high-priced products from foreign brands such as Alpinestars. They knew there was a big market for affordable, stylish and durable riding gear in India.

The third idea was to get into corporate gifting. They thought they could get some funky, customized gifting merchandise from China, where these items were available cheap. In late 2008, things like laptop cooling pads and mini can holders which could be powered by USB ports of laptops were all the rage.

Finally after much debate, they decided to get into the web-based services domain because the other two options called for huge investments. To enter the riding gear business and make a mark, they would need their own manufacturing facility. And that would mean putting up a capital investment of several crore rupees. The corporate gifting business, on the other hand, called for huge up-front payments to their manufacturers based in China. Not just that, they would also have to wait for four or five months, sometimes even longer, to get paid by their corporate clients.

The three friends firmly believed that they shouldn't have to invest huge amounts in order to set up or expand a business. A business that offered scope for growth and profitability without calling for big investments was the ideal deal as far as they were concerned. And that's how they decided to enter the Internet space.

Thus iGenero was born in the early days of 2009.

Aditya pauses to take a sip of his tea and to catch his breath. After a couple of minutes, I nudge him to resume his narration. I ask him what the name of his company means and how they hit upon it.

Aditya's explanation is simple. 'Genero' means 'create' in Latin. They added an 'i' to it to connote the focus on customization for their customers. Through the name, the team wanted to convey this message – 'We work on whatever idea is in your mind and create something beautiful out of it for your business.' A friend of his suggested this name.

They liked it because they thought it conveyed something simple and meaningful to their prospective clients. Also, it added a dash of sophistication to their venture. 'We thought it sounded good too, like a serious brand name,' says Aditya with a smile.

'We definitely did not want to name our company "XYZ Technology Solutions" or something like that. That would have been clichéd,' he adds.

But iGenero was not the first name they thought of for their company. Believe it or not, the first name they thought of was 'chaibiscuit.com'. They felt it was very different from the usual boring company names and was very funky. It had an air of informality which appealed to the easy-going nature of the three founders.

But a quick survey amongst people they knew told them that this was not the right name for their company. The people they spoke to thought that the name was too casual – almost frivolous – and that prospective customers would not take the company seriously. And so the name was dropped. However, not wanting to let go of the name completely, the trio bought the domain registration under that name. They still hold it. 'We will use it when we start a new service or a business that can take such a cool name,' says Aditya with a laugh.

Like every start-up, iGenero went through tough times initially. The three founders did not have enough money to take up office space. They did not want to borrow money from their parents either. That left the option of working from home (all of them were staying with their parents). They would take turns to work out of one another's homes every day. And at night, they would meet and strategize over chai. All their conversations at that time were about acquiring clients and their long-term dream for iGenero.

Getting projects was tough. The only service iGenero offered at that time was to create websites for companies. But there were many other companies which provided the same service! To add to that, none of the three founders had a technical knowledge of IT and the Internet. Aditya admits that to this day he can't write code. And finally, none of them had any corporate experience or reputation.

In sum, the question they were repeatedly asked by companies was, 'Why should we give this project to you? It is too risky for us.'

That was when the youngsters' social contacts came in handy. They posted about their new venture on their respective Facebook pages and informed other contacts as well. One day, a friend told them that Sweet Nirvana, a fine-dining Italian restaurant in Hyderabad, was looking for someone who could create the restaurant's website. The three musketeers met the owners and pitched for the project. 'We did not even have visiting cards at that time! Our cards had not been printed yet. We hadn't even designed our logo!' says an amused Aditya.

'We were desperate for that project. And we somehow managed to convince the client to give it to us. I just don't know how we pulled it off.' iGenero's first project was worth Rs 35,000, out of which they got Rs 17,000 as an advance to start the work with. The balance was to be paid on completion of the website. Since the company did not have a corporate bank account, the cheque for the advance was issued in Aditya's name.

Understandably, it was a sweet moment for the newly-minted entrepreneurs. Their joy knew no bounds. They were finally in business! The hunt for someone who could develop the website started. They tried hiring a couple of freelancers to do the job, but that attempt failed. Freelancers, they discovered, could not devote their attention to this project since they were working on a number of other projects at the same time.

Again the founders' contacts proved useful. They managed to rope in someone from Karan's erstwhile employer and get the job done.

The client was happy and paid them the balance amount. Having completed their first project, the founders' confidence went up a notch. They started scouting for more projects aggressively. Their first client did her bit by recommending iGenero to other people she knew.

The all-important question was, 'Where will the next client come from?' All the founders were outgoing people who had developed strong social networks through their families and college mates. These networks were to help them again – this would happen repeatedly in the future too. iGenero landed two more tiny projects soon after.

At this stage, the founders decided to regularize things at the company a little more. The first two things they wanted to do were to find a small office and to hire a full-time technical person. As luck would have it, Aditya's father was moving out of a small office and into a larger one. He persuaded the landlord to let the vacated space to iGenero at a reasonable rent. The office suited the tiny company's purposes. It needed just a little bit of cleaning and a small facelift. 'We wanted the office to look clean. We wanted young people to love working out of it.'

The facelift did not help much; at least, not immediately. When the founders advertised for their first employee, they found that many applicants were turned off by the location of the office (Suryakiran Complex, where the office was located, was an old and stale commercial complex in Secunderabad).

After a painful wait, they did get their first employee. Ganesh was very good at coding and was quite interested in joining iGenero. The founders hammered out a win-win deal and brought him on board. They got him a computer with the necessary technical specifications to get him started. Next they hired a designer. With a designer-developer team in place, they finally felt that they had a complete (though tiny) team for the time being. To develop websites, a designer-developer team is essential. While the designer conceptualizes the design of the website (including the colours, the look and feel), the developer takes care of the technical aspects like coding, creating back links, plugins, etc.

iGenero was now geared up to take on more projects. There was a new-found drive in the team. Explains Aditya, 'We were taking it step by step. We were not great risk takers. We believed in taking calculated decisions. And we were fine with the rate at which we were growing.'

More projects started coming in. They renovated the office a little more, made it hipper. Also, they started taking on small social media-related projects. By then iGenero had its own website too. Things were looking better.

Someone suggested that they convert their business from a partnership into a private limited company. Among other things, he said this would help the promoters raise funds through investments and loans when required. It would give them a lot of leverage with external stakeholders. Aditya and team immediately acted upon this suggestion.

The next big moment for the start-up came from a completely unexpected quarter. At the time of graduating from college, Aditya had applied to the George Washington University in the USA for admission to their master's programme. He got in, but deferred his date of joining. One day, the dean of the college wrote to him asking why he was deferring the admission repeatedly. Aditya promptly told her that he was now an entrepreneur and so could not pursue higher studies. He requested the dean to cancel his admission. The dean agreed and then asked him what business he was in. When he told her, she immediately asked him to send her a proposal for designing the social media presence for the engineering department of the university!

As soon as Aditya gathered his wits, he sent her the proposal. Two weeks later, iGenero was given the project. The entire team was speechless! The project brought them a sizeable monthly retainer; it was a very profitable one. George Washington University, Aditya tells me, is one of the biggest clients iGenero has had so far.

Bagging this project definitely marked an inflexion point in the evolution of the company. The trio felt that they could really make a dent in the market and carve out an identity for themselves. With George Washington University on their list of clients, their credibility went up quite a bit in the market.

'That was one of our Eureka moments,' says Aditya.

They roped in a friend from the advertising industry to join them as their social media consultant and handle the George Washington account.

By now word had spread about this enthusiastic and confident team. Projects kept coming in, mainly through client referrals and word-of-mouth. Aditya tells me that to this day, they have acquired 90 per cent of their clients this way. Only the balance 10 per cent have come through their sales efforts. 'Our past clients have vouched for our work – they have supported us very well. I am really grateful to them for that. Also, people saw the work we did for other clients and called us,' says Aditya. I can see that he is feeling emotional as he talks about how his clients have supported his company.

Obviously, not all projects have come to them easily. There have been many projects for which they have had to pitch and compete with other agencies. But that has only been in the case of certain big companies which invite proposals from different agencies and follow a multi-step process in awarding projects.

How did they feel dealing with Ganesh, their first employee, who was much older than them? The mood turns a little sombre as Aditya tells me that in some ways, they found it difficult to deal with him. The age gap always hung over them like a dark cloud. The owners were not comfortable with a much older person reporting to them. Moreover, Ganesh was from the old school of thought whereas the youngsters were in tune with the latest trends and developments. They were eager to make the most of any new technology that emerged in the market. Also, since Ganesh lived far away from the office, he was not keen to stay back and put in extra time to complete work. One day, he told the owners that he was quitting iGenero. They understood his dilemma and let him go. Not just that, they found him a good job in another company.

Soon, iGenero hired more people and beefed up its team. Learning from their experience with Ganesh, the company was careful about who it hired. All their newer team members came through known contacts only. In addition, to the greatest extent possible, they ensured that they hired people who were on more or less the same wavelength as them.

'We picked people who were informal and fun-loving yet good at work. Finding the right mindset was very important, we realized,' is how Aditya looks at it.

'And what effect has this approach had on the work culture at iGenero?' I ask.

'Thanks to our team, we have a great time at work. People wake up and come to office full of energy. Because our office is not like a typical office at all! All of us vibe very well with one another. We have a lot of fun at work. On most days all of us have lunch together, however late it may be. And someone or the other is always playing music on their computer.'

The entire team at iGenero is mature and responsible enough to know that the client's needs always come first. If that means someone has to stay back late into the night to finish work, they will. Many a time the founders themselves have stayed up with their team through the night to ensure that a client's project is completed and delivered the next morning.

'What about employee attrition?' I wonder aloud.

Practically zero, apparently. Aditya tells me that those who joined the company after its initial days have stayed with them until now. He attributes this to the kind of people they hired and to the work culture they have built in the company.

After eighteen months in the small office in Secunderabad, the company moved its base to Banjara Hills, a hip part of town. They could now afford the move. Since many of their clients were in this area, this move also made it easy to have regular meetings with them. The company continues to operate from this address.

In 2011, Armin decided to study business management and left the company. From then on, Karan and Aditya have been running the show. I ask Aditya how the two of them have divided work responsibilities. He tells me that while he looks after business development and marketing, Karan takes care of operations and finance. So Aditya is the man on the street while Karan is the one who holds down the fort.

I ask Aditya about their rate of expansion so far. Are he and Karan happy with it? Do they think they could have done better?

He answers candidly that their rate of growth is less than that of other companies in the same industry, but that they are not worried. They want to expand systematically, ensuring that they don't borrow money for expansion. While many friends and venture capitalists (VCs) have told them they could grow faster by borrowing money, Aditya and Karan have opted not to do so. Their style is to make a profit and plough it back into the business to fund its expansion – the classic bootstrapping approach.

It is a psychological thing too. Aditya says Karan and he will never sleep easy if they have borrowed huge sums of money from investors or from the bank. They would forever be wondering if they'd be able to repay the money.

Our conversation about growth brings another incident to Aditya's mind. An incident that marked the second inflexion point in iGenero's evolution. Karan and Aditya met a VC in early 2012. During the course of the meeting, he pointed out iGenero's strengths and weaknesses. He told them that with their competent and loyal team and a good set of clients, they were in a reasonably strong position. They did not suffer from the biggest problems that many of their competitors faced – high employee attrition and poor quality of work.

At the same time, the VC told them that they were under-pricing themselves. The prices they were quoting for projects were far lower than the ones being quoted by companies that were half as competent as iGenero. He advised them to analyse the pricing patterns in the industry and correct their own accordingly. To their great surprise, they found that they could increase iGenero's price considerably and still come across as being reasonable. The extent to which they had been under-valuing themselves became clear to Aditya and Karan. This was a real eye-opener.

With the increase in pricing, iGenero's billings and profits shot up accordingly. That too without any increase in the size of the team or the rest of their infrastructure. No doubt, the entrepreneurs were gleeful.

I ask him where iGenero stands today, after a six year journey.

Aditya is quietly happy as he tells me that the company is in a happy position today. It is confident about its future. Its work has been appreciated by clients and many others. They get new projects without too much difficulty. Their team is very competent, confident and loyal. All of them have fun at work and at the same time make a decent bit of money too. Recently, the annual turnover of the company touched the eight figure mark.

iGenero now has a twenty member team. It opened its Bengaluru office in 2014 and its Mumbai office in January 2015. Both these cities are huge markets for online branding, design and other web-based services. Delhi is their next destination.

In the same breath though, Aditya adds that the company is still a baby in the industry. It has a long, long way to go. There is so much more to learn. The fact that Karan and he are still very young – much younger than most of their clients – does bother them now and then. But not as much as it used to in their early days.

I am keen to know what Aditya thinks have been his and Karan's biggest learning experiences in their entrepreneurial journey.

He sits back and thinks for a minute before answering.

'The need for patience,' he says emphatically. 'At every stage our patience has been tested severely. During such times, in spite of the initial frustration and sadness, we have somehow always managed to come through. For instance, during the early days, the three of us did not draw any salary for ten or twelve months at a stretch. We kept thinking of our big dream, gritted our teeth and somehow pulled through that phase. And it has paid off.

'Another important lesson we learnt is that it is very important to keep clients happy through your work. If you do that, they will be more than happy to spread the word about your company's competence. This will invariably result in more business for your company.

'Getting the right team is vital too.

'And finally, my visit to Bombay was an eye-opener. I was zapped by the energy and work focus of the people there. Bombay taught me a lot about professionalism.'

SIDELIGHTS

- Aditya is a passionate biker and the proud owner of a Royal Enfield Bullet. He has ridden to Ladakh with his biking club. He gets out of the city every so often and roams around to recharge his batteries.

- Karan, on the other hand, is a movie fiend. He is in love with the art of storytelling, be it through books or through movies. Mentoring and teaching come naturally to him; people keep seeking him out for advice.

Aditya and Karan's Message to Young Entrepreneurs

- Try to visualize your future as much as you can. Think five-ten years ahead. See if what you are doing today relates to your vision.
- Evolve with the market. Don't stick to just one particular product or service. You have to evolve to stay in the race.
- Focus on people. They are the most important resource you have. Create a culture of belonging, a culture where people take ownership of their work and enjoy what they do. That is when you can get the most out of your team.
- There will be good days and there will be bad days. Forget the bad days, but at the same time, don't get carried away by the good days.

Key Learnings from Aditya and Karan's Story

- No venture operates in a vacuum. Therefore, constantly keep benchmarking your company against your competitors. This benchmarking has to be done on some important aspects like quality of work, services

offered, pricing, delivery timelines, etc. This will ensure that you are in tune with what's happening around you and adapt accordingly.
- The most important decision you'll have to take right at the beginning is which business/industry to enter. Decide only after you have analysed all the options available to you. Try to pick a business domain that you have a flair for, something that you can do well and enjoy doing.
- Borrow money for your business only if you are truly comfortable with the concept and if you are sure you will return the money to the lenders on time. Otherwise, bootstrap.
- Everybody has a different appetite for risk and growth. Set your goals according to this. There is no point in trying to copy somebody else's ambition and growth path.

8. Om Shanti Traders Bengaluru

Founder: Swati Bondia
Name of the company: Om Shanti Traders
Brand name: Om Shanti
Nature of business: Crafting and selling ethnic Indian objects of art.
Founded in: 2011
Based in: Bengaluru
Team size: Thirty-two
Vision for the business: To empower the underprivileged people of India by helping them earn their livelihood. In doing so, to bridge the gap between the different social classes as much as possible.
URL: www.omshantitraders.com

This story began on the streets. Literally. Coming from a family where everyone breathes, eats and sleeps business, it was but natural that Swati should take to business at a very early age. She grew up watching her dad manage his business and handle his employees effectively. Much later, she realized that he was what people called an 'entrepreneur'!

Setting up Om Shanti Traders in December 2011, she took to business like a fish takes to water.

With a disarming mix of humility, empathy and pragmatism, Swati is trying to do her bit for society while building a scalable, profitable enterprise at the same time. She has had her share of battles, but has fought her way through them.

STATE-OF-THE-ART

Swati was studying Bachelor of Business Management (BBM) at Acharya Institute of Management and Science in Peenya, Bengaluru. One evening in November 2011, she found herself stuck in an auto at a traffic signal in the Banashankari area of Bengaluru. A little girl, who looked to be all of five, came to her and begged for money. When Swati refused to give her anything, the girl started crying. Taking pity on her, Swati bought her some food and clothes and was about to send her home when the child asked for Rs 500. A shocked Swati asked the kid why she wanted the money. Upon hearing this, the child said that if she did not take money back home (as she was supposed to everyday), she would be thrashed by her mother. Apparently, the girl's brother was given the same task as well and suffered the same fate if he returned home empty-handed.

Too shocked to know what to do, Swati found herself asking the little girl to take her to her parents. Reaching the girl's hovel, Swati found her father drunk and her mother dishevelled and deeply despondent. Over the next few minutes, the family's tale of woes came tumbling out. They had apparently come to Bengaluru because a company had promised them work. But on arriving, they were shocked to find that the work did not materialize as promised. Local workers had come together and made it clear to the company that migrants were not to be given jobs. And so, the family found itself on the streets.

Deeply touched by their tale and the state of helplessness of the family, Swati's first thought was that she should help them in some way. But handing out money was out of the question. It would help the family only for a day or two but what after that? She wanted to see if she could find a more lasting solution. And so, after giving Shivu, the girl's father, a verbal lashing for hitting the bottle, she went to Peenya Industrial Estate (near her college), met a few companies there and sought work for Shivu and his wife. Unfortunately, no company was willing to give them any. A dejected Swati did not know what to do. As much as she wanted to help the family, she found she had run into a brick wall. When she went back to the hovel to deliver the bad news, she was taken aback. The entire family looked washed and clean. They, including Shivu, had put on whatever clean clothes they had and were eagerly awaiting news about work! Swati was surprised and emotionally touched. It was then that she took the decision that would change her life and theirs too. 'I thought that if I can't find them work in some other company, I would try to give them some work myself. I wanted to make them self-dependent.'

Swati decided that she would start a business of making and selling ethnic artefacts. The idea came to her from what she had seen back home in Orissa. Swati grew up seeing a number of beautiful ethnic art objects at home. Her sisters-in-law and other women at home used to make these objects themselves. It was a great way for them to pass the time. Marwari women in general have a keen sense of art and aesthetics. Across India, one can find a number of Marwari households adorned with ethnic artefacts, many of which have been made by the women of the house!

The first step was to undergo training in the art and science of making these artefacts. Swati and Shivu started small. They attended a two-week training workshop in Bengaluru. There, they learnt how to work with clay and model it into different shapes, how to make moulds, how to work with colour combinations, how to glaze the products, etc. In other words, Clay Modelling 101. At the end of the workshop, both of them felt confident enough to make small artefacts by themselves.

The very next day, Swati went to Shivaji Nagar, a major market in central Bengaluru. She had Rs 250 in her pocket, which she spent on the raw materials needed to make a statue of a Laughing Buddha. They made the statue and tried to sell it off of a pavement. Throughout the day, several people saw the statue, but no one showed any interest in buying it. After standing on the pavement for several hours, they finally managed to sell it for Rs 750. They had made their first sale and pocketed a profit of a cool Rs 500! Not bad at all considering the trying circumstances under which the piece had been made and sold.

The next day they went to another market in the Majestic area of the city and invested the entire profit earned the previous day in buying more of the same kind of materials. They made a few more Laughing Buddha statues and took them from house to house in Banashankari. By nightfall, they had managed to sell all the idols and make a tidy profit.

Over the next few days, Swati and Shivu settled into a daily work routine. All day, Shivu would make different kinds of statues while Swati attended her BBM classes. In the evening, both of them would take the idols from door to door and sell them. Usually, they would manage to sell most of their pieces but sometimes they would be left with some unsold ones. By and large though, they were happy that people liked the idols and were willing to pay for them. There was a good bit of haggling (which transaction in India does not involve haggling?!), but in the end, Swati managed to sell the idols for a decent price. 'We started small. I knew we were selling only simple stuff. But I wanted to be sure that the stuff we were making was of good quality, something durable.'

As the weeks went by, their daily revenue stabilized to within a certain range. Swati would give most of the profits to Shivu and keep a small portion for herself. She was happy that Shivu now had means to a living and was able to now support his family. Sometime later, Shivu and his family moved out of their hovel and into a single room tenement. They were able to afford two decent meals every day. Most importantly, he and his wife had now begun to think of sending their kids to school – a dream that had no place in their lives even a couple of months ago!

Swati now wanted to push the bar a little higher. She decided that they would make larger statues and other objects such as sculptures of deities. She asked her sisters to send her pictures of some of the things they had made at home. Her sisters also guided her in a lot of technical aspects such as making the moulds, mixing the colours right and getting the right consistency of the clay. 'I must thank Google Chat for making all this happen. Without it, I would never have learnt so much in such a short time!' says Swati.

I ask her if she ever thought of taking money from her parents to fund her business. Being a student and living on pocket money, was she not tempted to go to them for more money? 'My parents had done enough for me, I felt. I did not want to ask them for money any more. I thought it was high time I started making some by myself.'

Swati was clear that, at least for some time, all investments into her business would come from accrued profits only – the classic old-school model of bootstrapping which many famous entrepreneurs swear by.

Soon, Swati and Shivu were able to expand their product range to thirty-eight items which they continued selling from door to door. By now they had acquired a few repeat customers, some of whom had referred them to their friends. A few customers wanted objects made according to their specifications. The sharp businesswoman that she is, Swati agreed and made customized artefacts for them.

'We would make all the products by hand. We did not have the money to invest in machines or even rent them.'

Barely a month and a half after she sold her first Laughing Buddha came the first inflexion point for her business. One of her customers was part of a committee which was organizing an exhibition of art and craft products at Palace Grounds, Bengaluru. The customer gave Swati a 50 per cent discount on stall hire charges. She grabbed the deal and displayed her best products at the exhibition. While she did not sell much, her efforts definitely caught the attention of visitors. Her enterprise got some mileage. Also, she met a number of other artisans at the exhibition and learnt several nuances about creating objects of art from them. She made new business connections too. One specific thing she remembers learning from someone at the exhibition was that she could register her venture with the Ministry of Small and Medium Enterprises (MSME). That would help her venture establish its credentials to prospective customers.

The tremendous exposure she received at the exhibition also got Swati thinking about the long-term future of her venture. She realized that while the main reason she got into this business was somewhat charitable in nature, she would have to ensure that her venture was profitable. Only then would it be possible to sustain it, create more jobs and make sure that her efforts had a lasting and ever-increasing impact on society. A venture that does not make money helps nobody. It simply folds up in due course.

A day after Christmas in 2011, Swati registered her company as Om Shanti Traders under the MSME. She got a certificate from the ministry, a certificate she could use to bag orders.

While mulling over the option to expand the business, she realized that she should start targeting corporates for bulk orders. Selling to individual customers had two problems:

One, each order was for one or two pieces. The revenue size and profitability of each order was therefore very small.

Two, the company would have to sell to hundreds of individual customers in order to make a meaningful profit. This would mean an enormous effort in targeting prospective customers and convincing them to buy.

Corporate deals on the other hand, would be more manageable and profitable. In one shot, the company could sell a few hundred products to a single corporate customer. Corporates would buy them mainly as gifts for their employees and business associates.

Swati started calling up and sending emails to companies. But landing the first order was anything but easy. On the contrary, the story of how Swati bagged her first order is a lesson in persistence.

Among the first few companies she wrote to was a five star hotel called The Leela Palace. As it often happens when one is cold calling (or cold mailing in this case), one does not know exactly who to speak or write to. So one visits the website of the company in question, ferrets out an email id or two and shoots off a few emails to them. That is exactly what happened with Swati. She wrote to the customer care department of the hotel, describing her company and its products, and requesting an appointment with the general manager (GM) of the hotel. She figured out that in the case of a hotel like this, the GM would be the key decision maker.

Two days went by without a reply. Swati called the reception desk of the hotel, introduced herself and told the lady at the other end of the line that she wanted to meet the GM. The lady scoffed and told her that the GM was a very busy man and that there was a long queue of people waiting to meet him. She asked Swati to write to the marketing team of the hotel, which Swati did immediately.

Her mail to the marketing department was met with deafening silence. Swati was deeply disappointed. She did not know who else to contact at the hotel. After a week of waiting for a reply to her second mail, she went to the hotel. There, she met the receptionist, told him the tale and once again asked that she be put in touch with the GM. She was given the cold shoulder yet again. Thoroughly frustrated, Swati returned home and shot off an emotional mail to the marketing department, addressing her mail to the GM. She had practically given up on this case, but just wanted to give the hotel's GM and staff a piece of her mind.

This time however something clicked. Much to her surprise, she received a reply the very next day – that too, from none less than the GM himself. He asked Swati to meet him at the hotel the next week.

Swati remembers being very nervous as she walked into the GM's room the first time. 'I really didn't know what I was going to tell him. I was just operating on adrenaline.' She laughs as she recalls the tense moment. Once in the GM's room, she told him everything about what she was trying to achieve through Om Shanti Traders. It was not a very coherent or structured sales pitch, but definitely a very passionate one.

What she said piqued the interest of the GM. He started asking questions about the business model, the artisans who were making the products, her plans for the future, etc. As she went about answering his questions, various ideas came to her for the first time and the blueprint for the expansion of her business wrote itself out in her head! She remembers returning to her office later that day and jotting down those ideas and thoughts in her diary.

The GM, Mr Rao, heard Swati out, but was reluctant to place an order with her company. After all, Om Shanti Traders was a fledgling organization whereas The Leela Palace was one of the most reputed hotels in Bengaluru. What would the internal auditors of the hotel say when they found out that the hotel had placed an order with an unknown vendor? But Swati pleaded with him to give her a chance. In reply, he asked her to convince him about the quality of her products within twenty-four hours.

It was a make-or-break twenty-four hours for Swati. She racked her brains to find a way out. Finally, she approached Archies, the gifting store chain which was stocking her products at a few branches. She asked them to endorse the quality of her products. They were happy to give her a Certificate of Quality. The next day she met Mr Rao at The Leela with this certificate and a few more of her products. Swati showed him a Laughing Buddha and sold to him the idea of gifting it to clients, employees and business associates.

At the end of what seemed a lifetime to Swati, he decided to give her that all-important chance. He placed an order for 500 idols of the Laughing Buddha. Swati was speechless. Realization dawned on her that Om Shanti Traders had bagged its first ever corporate order!

But her ordeal was not over yet. The entire lot had to be delivered to The Leela Palace in eight days. With just one artisan on her team, making 500 idols in eight days was impossible! Swati would need many more artisans to help. Also, she would have to get the raw materials very quickly so that work could start the very next day. And to get the raw materials and hire artisans, she would need money. Which she did not have. She asked The Leela for an advance, but the hotel refused. It was not their policy to give vendors an advance, they said. Taking pity on her plight, the GM gave her a loan of Rs 30,000 from his own pocket.

Thanking her stars (and the GM, of course!), Swati set about marshalling her resources. She roped in twenty-five extra artisans for this project and closely supervised their work. The team worked day and night to craft the pieces. The eight days passed in a heartbeat and the 500 idols were finally, miraculously, ready. Each idol was packed carefully and the entire lot was delivered to the hotel four hours before the promised time. A beaming GM ensured that the hotel released her payment for the order promptly and also gave Om Shanti Traders a Certificate of Appreciation. Swati gratefully repaid his loan and thanked him for all his help.

Nothing short of a miracle, right? Maybe, but Swati had a hand in making the miracle happen. If she had not persisted in her effort to get through to the GM and had given up hope early on, the miracle would never have happened. Something to think about.

Swati singles out The Leela Palace episode as the one incident that swung the fortune of her company. It taught her the value of persistence and serendipity. It taught her to think on her feet in response to dire circumstances. Lastly, it taught her that come what may, she had it in her to pull it off!

The next corporate order came from her college, Acharya Institute of Management and Science. The college wanted 200 pieces of a miniature sculpture as a symbol of good luck. She delivered this order on time too.

The principal was pleased no end, especially since a student of her own college was involved. Swati now knew that she had acquired a foothold in the hospitality and education industries. She wrote to other leading hotels and colleges in Bengaluru and landed a few more bulk orders.

Since then, the company has focused on corporate orders only. However, from time to time Swati decides to serve individual customers but only those who were her earliest customers. She feels sentimentally attached to them. 'They were the ones who helped us make a beginning, even if it was only a humble beginning. I feel I owe it to them.'

Growing steadily, Om Shanti Traders acquired a pile of surplus cash. A few months ago, the company invested that money in buying some essential machinery. These machines help turn out products faster and of much higher quality standards. Swati sees this as a big step forward. While she does not want to get into the mass manufacture of artefacts, she definitely wants to achieve a certain level of scale and speed, for which machines would be vital. Like all professional set-ups, Om Shanti Traders now uses machines for moulding, painting, mixing and grinding.

Ever since the machines have come in, the monthly profits of the company have improved.

Om Shanti Traders now has a workshop in Banashankari and a warehouse in Peenya, both in Bengaluru. Also, the company has roped in eight more artisans.

Swati's work has won her a lot of appreciation and accolades. In 2012, she was named the best student entrepreneur in Bengaluru by the Aditya Birla Group. More recently (in mid-2013) the Gujarat National Law University awarded Swati the 'Bauribandhu Mohapatra & GNLU Community Service Award' for community service. She went to Gujarat to collect this award, which was handed over to her by Narendra Modi, the then chief minister of Gujarat (now prime minister of India).

Plans are on to open a branch of Om Shanti Traders in Gujarat, the funds for which will come from the state's government. A similar branch is already running in Orissa, funded by the Government of Orissa. The fact that the state governments are willing to partner with Swati is proof of the potential the governments see in an effort of this kind. They realize that Om Shanti Traders is founded on a very noble principle. Yet, at the same time, the company has built a scalable, replicable model for the business.

Swati is extremely grateful to her college and in particular to the Acharya Entrepreneurship Excellence Centre (AEEC) run by the college. She credits AEEC, its director, Professor Ranganathan, and Professor B.M. Ramamurthy for giving her venture its early impetus. 'They used to spend a lot of time with me, giving me useful suggestions for the business. They encouraged me to continue on this journey. Also, the mentoring programmes run by AEEC helped me think professionally.'

Other major influences, Swati says, are Professor Sourav Mukherjee, who teaches inclusive business models at IIM Bengaluru and Dr Kerron Reddy, the chairperson of her college. Along with them is, of course, her father Mr Subash Kumar Bondia, the person who first inspired her to strike out on her own. He has been with her every step of the way, guiding and motivating her.

For quite some time after she set up Om Shanti Traders, her family and friends had no idea that she was running a business. It was through an amusing turn of events that her parents found out. Swati and her efforts had been getting a good bit of coverage in the press in Bengaluru. One day, an enterprising reporter from the *Times of India* tracked down her parents' phone number and called them up. Her dad took the call. The reporter asked him what he thought of the work his daughter was doing. 'But she's just studying management,' her father said. 'Oh, no! I am asking about the other thing she is doing,' returned the reporter. 'What other thing?' asked her dad, completely puzzled. And that was when the reporter told him about Swati's venture. The news pleased her father very much and he happily shared it with her mother. Both of them (and soon enough, the entire family) felt proud that one of their own was an independent businesswoman, doing her bit to help the poor. Normally, in Marwari families, it is the men who take to business. They bring home the bacon while the women run the household. By and large, you don't find women taking up a job, let alone running their own businesses.

Swati is fortunate to have been born to parents who are progressive in thought. Rather than take her to task for doing something on her own, they appreciated her work and encouraged her to build the business further. And she is deeply thankful for this. These days, when she goes home on a break, the whole family peppers her with questions about her business. Everyone is keen to know of the latest developments and the latest orders.

And unknowingly, Swati has become a role model for the girls of her community. A few of them are keen to become entrepreneurs, following in her footsteps. Also, the elders in the family no longer hesitate to send their daughters to another city for higher education – this was unthinkable earlier.

'Atta girl!' is all one can say.

SIDELIGHTS

- When she feels stressed because of her hectic schedule, Swati takes off on long drives. She loves to explore new routes and stops here and there to talk to farmers and roadside vendors. This calms her down and gives her a new perspective on life.
- In 2014, Swati was the only participant to be chosen from the SAARC countries for the Bottom of the Pyramid Challenge, a global contest supported by the UN. She went to the University of Columbia in Bogota to attend this contest.
- In 2014, Om Shanti Traders set up a training arm called Focus. This educates rural and underprivileged people on the subject of entrepreneurship and helps them become entrepreneurs too.

Swati's Message to Young Entrepreneurs

- Just live life to the fullest. Do what you feel like doing and don't go by what others say. Even if they say that your thoughts or ideas will lead you in the wrong direction, *you* decide for yourself. Make your own path. Nobody but you can see your own path. Sometimes, you may fail. But then failures teach you valuable lessons. Learn the lessons and never repeat a mistake.
- Life is actually very simple. It is our mind that complicates matters.

Key Learnings from Swati's Story

- In any enterprise, human capital is the biggest asset.
- Getting the first big break is usually very difficult for a start-up. Don't give up, keep trying – like Swati did with The Leela Palace. Her perseverance finally paid off. The first few opportunities are hard to get. So when you do get them, put in your heart and soul. Later on, life will become a little simpler.

9. Center Stage
Pune

Founder: Avik Bhattacharya
Name of the company: Center Stage Dance Company
Brand name: Center Stage
Nature of business: Training in dance; plans to extend/move into other performing arts soon.
Founded in: 2012
Based in: Pune
Team size: Nine
Vision for the business: To provide dance enthusiasts with comprehensive artistic education that fosters excellence. And to make dance a lifestyle hobby, thereby urging people to lead healthier and happier lives.
URL: www.facebook.com/pages/Center-Stage-Where-Artists-Belong/553334741359681

Had he not become a dance artist, what would Avik Bhattacharya be doing? Most probably, nothing.

Born into a family that loves the arts, Avik's entire childhood was suffused with the colour and joy of cinema, theatre and music. No wonder then that it seeped into him and took over his soul over a period of time.

When the time came for him to decide what to do in life, he very naturally chose to do something in the world of the arts. He chose to build his professional identity in the arena of dance by setting up a dance academy.

As he single-mindedly goes about trying to make more people dance to his tunes, he is clearly having the time of his life!

Dance Like a Man

As I step up to shake hands with Avik Bhattacharya, I take in his slim and toned physique. His movements are easy and graceful, as you would expect of a dancer.

Having spoken to Avik over the phone and read up about him earlier, I know that his life has been like a laser beam with a steady and sharply focused path. Right from the beginning, his life has been dominated by the performing arts. Speaking to him now, I get the feeling that deep in his heart, he knew all along that his destiny lay in this field. And so, without much ado, I ask him when and how his love affair with dance began.

Flashback time!

Avik's mom, Mrs Lily Bhattacharya, is a Bengali lyricist and stage actress while his dad, Mr Ajay Bhattacharya, writes screenplays and dialogue for Bengali theatre and films. He wrote the story and script for a Bengali film called *Chopper* which was screened at the Russian Film Festival in

1986. Since theatre was the couple's shared passion, Mr Bhattacharya set up his theatre troupe 'Bringhon' in 2002.

Very soon their house in Kolkata became an 'adda'. Think of it as a heady cocktail of friends, stimulating conversations, chai and a strong dose of 'atmosphere'. Many film, music and theatre artistes would spend hours in Avik's house discussing art-related matters over numerous cups of chai. 'I felt as though my whole being had been taken over by theatre, films and music. These things were all around me!' Avik recalls animatedly.

I ask him how he was introduced to dance. It turns out that Avik learnt Kathak for five years when he was in school. He realized that he had a natural sense of rhythm; his body intuitively understood how to move gracefully and with economy of movement which is so vital for a dancer. Slowly he fell in love with dance. And what about the art forms his parents had embraced? Did he not feel like pursuing those? 'Of course, I loved theatre, films and music. I love all the art forms even today. But I just wanted to try out dance first because it was different from what I had been seeing at home. Somehow, I was most passionate about dance. I wanted to explore it.'

I realize that trying to decode Avik's love for dance would be pointless. There isn't an exact, rational reason for his strong attraction to it. His love for dance is something he has felt in his bones for a long time. Something that has perhaps always been there subliminally. It happens to all of us at some point of time or the other. We feel passionately about things without being able to say exactly why. But when we encounter that something face-to-face, we are simply transported. We lose ourselves in the experience. Passion therefore is an intensely personal and subjective thing. Often, inexplicable.

And so it is with Avik and dancing.

After coming to Pune in 2004 to study aeronautical engineering, he continued his tryst with dancing. He joined Shiamak Davar's dance academy and learnt Bollywood jazz, hip-hop and contemporary dance. 'Getting into modern dance forms was so exhilarating. In these, the movements are so different from those in the classical forms of dance,' is how Avik puts it. With his natural flair, Avik made it to Shiamak's small group of high-potential dancers.

The high point of his time at Shiamak's dance academy was performing at the closing ceremony of the Commonwealth Youth Games, which was held in Pune in 2006. Avik describes that experience in one word – 'mind-blowing'. Apart from having a great time dancing in front of millions of people, he made a lot of friends in the dance troupe.

The two years spent at Shiamak's dance academy taught Avik so much more than just dance. It taught him professionalism, something he would find invaluable when he turned entrepreneur later.

Unfortunately, Avik's dance training came to a halt in late 2007. Not having the money to pay for his dance classes, he had to take a break from Shiamak's academy. He did not want to take more money from his elderly parents. In any case, they were already paying for his college education. He knew that staying away from dance classes was going to break his heart, but he had no choice. Desperate to return to dance as soon as possible, he thought of ways to raise the necessary funds. The only option was to work somewhere in a part-time role. That way he could attend classes in college during the day and work in the evenings and possibly even on weekends.

And that is what he ended up doing. For the next two and a half years, Avik worked as a trainer at a few Business Process Outsourcing (BPO) companies in Pune. As a trainer in language, voice and accent, he had to teach his students the nuances of the English language, accents, voice modulation, inflexion, etc. A far cry from dancing indeed!

I ask him how it felt to be standing in one shot conducting training workshops, in contrast to experiencing the exhilaration of dance. 'Bad, very bad,' says Avik, without batting an eyelid. 'My friends in the dancing fraternity would keep asking me to leave this job and get back to dancing. But I knew I could not do that for some time at least. I used to feel very sad.'

It was not as though Avik completely lost touch with dance during this phase. He would dance in his room and often get together with a few friends to do a gig. Dance was his life's breath and nothing could keep him from it.

The training assignments fetched Avik about Rs 13,000 a month. Avik put away every precious rupee he earned as a trainer. He knew he was building a nestegg which would help him fund his dream of being a professional dancer.

In June 2010, he finally realized that he could not take it anymore. He simply *had* to quit his job and take up dancing on a full-time basis again. He started reaching out to his dancer friends and scouting for a suitable opening. Soon enough, he got one. Mrudang Academy for Excellence in Creative Arts, a well-known dance institute in Pune, asked him to conduct a workshop. Post the workshop, he was taken on as a dance trainer at the same institute and told he would be paid Rs 200 per hour of training.

After joining Mrudang, Avik realized that the academy had some rough edges which he could help smooth out. For instance, he saw that the salsa being taught at Mrudang was basic and not technically correct. Having learnt salsa himself, Avik knew that if Mrudang could teach the dance form in its authentic style, there would be far more students. Salsa had caught the fancy of people across the globe. In India too, this dance form was highly aspirational amongst youngsters. Most people think of it as a glamorous, highly social and cool dance form.

He spoke to the owners of Mrudang about this and as a result brought in a few young trainers he knew. One of them was an expert in salsa while another was a master of the technique of popping locking. ('Popping' refers to the act of quickly contracting and relaxing your muscles, causing a jerk in your body. These jerks are known as pops or hits. 'Locking' involves performing a quick movement, segueing into another position and then holding the last position for a few seconds. These movements are synchronized with the beats of the music.) Mrudang therefore started teaching authentic salsa with all its variations. As for Avik himself, he started teaching hip-hop, Bollywood dance and contemporary dance.

Avik also realized that certain new dimensions could be added to Mrudang's offerings. For instance, Mrudang only conducted dance classes *within* its premises. It had never ventured outside to conduct classes. But Avik knew that there were a lot of people across the city of Pune who would be interested in learning modern dance forms. Pune is a city of colleges, IT and ITES organizations. A large percentage of the city's population is made up of young people. And young people are interested in dancing! So, Avik thought, why couldn't Mrudang seek out these young people across the city and conduct dance classes for them at their place of work or study?

That is how he hit upon the idea of tying up with corporates and colleges to conduct dance classes for their employees and students respectively. The idea proved to be a hit! Further, he got Mrudang opportunities to conduct dance shows in companies on special occasions like corporate parties, anniversaries, product launches, etc.

Finally, using his connections Avik helped Mrudang open two new centres in Pune – one at Swargate and the other at Karve Nagar. All of this improved Mrudang's business considerably. It increased the reach and visibility of the academy too and helped it enter new segments in the market for dance.

And so, having joined Mrudang as a dance trainer, Avik quickly took on other responsibilities. Soon however, he reached a point of saturation. He found that he did not have anything new to explore or learn at Mrudang. Also, now that its business had increased manifold, Mrudang's owners had their hands full. They could not expand further for some time to come. They had to focus on consolidating their existing business.

For a restless and adrenaline pumped person like Avik, the excitement levels started to fall at Mrudang. Another troubling factor was his salary. Avik found that, in spite of his contribution to Mrudang, he was not getting paid enough. He felt that he definitely deserved more.

One day, he saw a poster for a dance academy called Naach. He promptly called them up and spoke to Girish, a senior trainer there. Girish called him over for a meeting. When they met, Girish told Avik that Naach was looking for a dance trainer who specialized in contemporary and Bollywood style dancing. When he found that Avik had trained in these two forms, he was happy. He put Avik in touch with Abhilasha and Rohit, the owners of Naach. Avik told Abhilasha and Rohit that he had trained several children in the past too and that he could help Naach specialize in kids' dance if they were interested. And interested they were!

The decision was taken quickly. Avik joined Naach as a dance instructor at a pay of Rs 350 per hour of training. Naach offered a wide range of dance forms. Girish mainly focused on Latin, salsa, casino rueda and bachata – dance forms that had a strong Latin influence, having originated in Latin America.

Joining Naach, Avik started taking specialized classes for kids. Apart from that he also taught Bollywood, contemporary and hip-hop for adults. Learning of his good networking shills, Abhilasha gave him the additional responsibility of bringing in new business for Naach.

Avik took on the role of head – business development at Naach with gusto. Among the various deals he struck for Naach, he remembers getting a contract to choreograph the Sangeet ceremony of a socialite's wedding.

Soon Naach started conducting dance workshops and regular training sessions for companies like Infosys, TCS, Barclays, Vodafone and Kalpataru Builders. In between, Avik trained in Zumba, the hot new sensation on the dance floor and then started teaching it at Naach.

Phew! I can see that Avik was in the thick of things at Naach. The institute seemed to have tapped his creative instincts, his high level of energy and his passion for dance, thereby keeping him occupied and in a happy state of mind. The institute's revenues too kept growing.

I ask Avik to pick his best contribution to Naach. In other words, that one thing he feels happiest about when he thinks of his stint at Naach.

'It has to be BFAB. No doubt about that,' says Avik.

Born from a Boom Box (BFAB), the first stage show organized by Naach, was Avik's brainchild. Naach had never before organized something like it. Avik thought it would be a good idea to get the students and trainers of Naach onstage and showcase their dancing repertoire to the city of Pune. The show would help prove Naach's dancing credentials to the city as a whole and would bring in some money too. The first BFAB was organized in August 2011. It was a sell-out. The audience loved the performances so much that the Naach team was keen to organize another edition of the event. The second show was conducted in December 2011. This time the demand for tickets was higher. Having heard about the first BFAB, people were keen to see more of the same this time.

Both editions of BFAB were ticketed events and earned Naach a decent amount of money which the company could plough back into the institute.

Around this time, Avik spoke to the owners of Naach about making the academy a more professional set-up. He felt that it could and should transform itself into a complete education centre for dance and should not be just another academy like so many others.

He felt Naach, with its repertoire of dance forms, its excellent instructors and growing reputation, had the potential to position itself a few notches higher than where it stood at that time.

I ask Avik about the kind of improvements he had had in mind for the academy. 'For starters, I thought Naach should be incorporated formally as a company. That itself would bring in more seriousness in the owners and other team members. Then we could have created specialized teams such as a team of choreographers, a team of fitness instructors, a performance squad, etc.'

The underlying objective, I can make out, was to explore the untapped opportunities in the market.

He broached the idea with Abhilasha and Rohit, the owners. While they seemed interested in the idea, they did not implement his suggestions. Avik was left frustrated. He realized that if he wanted to achieve his vision of creating a 'complete' dance academy, he would have to take matters into his hands. In other words, he would have to set up his own dance academy.

For a while, Avik had been thinking of enrolling in a business management programme, considering it would help him run his dance academy whenever he set it up. He wrote the entrance exams in late 2011 and got admission to Indira School of Business Studies, Pune. The course started in July 2012. As soon as it started, Avik became a part-time employee at Naach. He went to college during the day and took dance classes at the academy in the evenings.

At the same time, he started jotting down thoughts and ideas about the dance academy he wanted to set up. 'I told myself I could become the best only if I did things myself.'

The same month (July 2012), Avik conducted a trial batch of sorts under the name Center Stage. He did this merely to see if he could handle a batch well and be a good trainer, solely on his own merit. He found that he did well; the students were happy with the way he conducted the dance sessions.

Emboldened, Avik spoke to a few close dancer friends about setting up an independent dance academy. He liked the name Center Stage and decided to retain it.

He knew he did not need much capital to start with – at least, to make a small but solid beginning. He could take a small place on rent and conduct the classes there. As and when each centre stabilized, he could add more centres. At the same time, he could approach corporates and colleges and offer to conduct dance classes on their premises for their employees and students respectively. Not just that, gyms and health clubs have begun offering dance as part of their fitness training routine. They are happy to partner with dance instructors and conduct dance sessions. Should he choose one of these avenues, Avik knew he would avoid a lot of unnecessary capital investment – after all, he would not have to put down money for a rental deposit or for furnishing the interiors.

Convinced he could create a sustainable business out of this idea, he wrote out a business plan. He participated in a few inter-collegiate B-Plan competitions and won a couple of them.

All this while, he had been in touch with many of his friends and associates in the dance fraternity. Girish, his colleague at Naach, was one of them. Girish told Avik that he was not happy at Naach because he was not growing professionally. His earnings weren't increasing either and he was mulling over moving out.

Avik invited Girish to join hands with him and help him set up his dance academy. Girish was only too happy! Their coming together was good because each of them specialized in different dance forms.

Together, they could offer a wide range of dance forms, thereby attracting more students than they would have otherwise.

Both of them left Naach in January 2013. They sat down and grappled with important questions regarding their dance academy like:

How would they stand out from a host of dance institutes in the market?

How would they hold their own against established biggies like Shiamak Davar, Rocky Poonawala and Naach?

What is the market potential?

What kind of team should they put together?

From where would they recruit their team?

How could they quickly scale up operations?

And many other questions like these.

That same month, the business plan for Center Stage was selected as one of the top twenty-one business plans at the Tata First Dot Contest. For this achievement, Avik gives all credit to his friend Yash Lohiya, who is a business consultant and a Latin ballroom dance instructor. Center Stage received a lot of attention from the media for making it to the top in this contest. He also thanks National Entrepreneurship Network (NEN), which is the lead organization behind the Tata First Dot Contest. NEN mentored him well and helped him improve a lot of aspects of his venture.

Mitali Kulkarni, a friend of Avik's, was then the dance teacher at Indira National School. She suggested that Avik and Girish open their first branch in the Pimple–Saudagar area of Pune because a lot of young people working in IT and ITES companies lived there. Also, this area did not have any good dance institutes.

The two partners started looking for a suitable place in the area to open their first branch. Simultaneously, they were working feverishly to put a host of other elements in place. They bought the domain name www.centerstagedance.in, got a logo designed for the academy and created a Facebook page for it too. They had leaflets designed and distributed them in Pimple-Saudagar. All this entailed an initial investment of Rs 45,000 which was taken from Avik's savings.

In February 2013, Center Stage opened its first branch at Optimum Health Gymnasium. Avik and Girish organized a two-hour demo session on 9 February to give people a preview of the dance styles that Center Stage would offer. 150 people attended this session and most of them ended up joining the academy. In the very first month, Center Stage took in ninety-six students across four different dance styles.

Finally they were in business! Avik's dream of running his own dance academy had come true. He was now an entrepreneur. He was jumping for joy!

I mull over Avik's incredible journey for a moment and then shoot my next question at him. Has he been able to differentiate Center Stage from other dance institutes? If yes, how?

Avik's answer is emphatically in the affirmative. He says that he simply recalled the lessons in professionalism he had imbibed at Shiamak Davar's institute and got down to implementing them at Center Stage. Most importantly, he has asked the dance instructors at Center Stage to maintain a strictly professional relationship with the students of the academy. He has issued a set of guidelines for the instructor-student relationship, one of which says that no instructor should share his/her phone number with a student and vice versa.

Next, his instructors do not simply teach people to dance. They talk to their students about its history, the evolution of a particular dance form, the social and cultural influences that have gone into shaping it, etc. In other words, they give students a whole new perspective on the dance form they are learning.

Another subtle but important touch is to ask students to use dance-related terms when they talk to one another about dance. Finally, students have been given a short set of simple dos and don'ts (for instance, 'Please bring a hand towel and deodorant', 'Please do not smoke or drink in the premises') which they have to follow when they come for class.

So far, Center Stage has set up eight centres in Pune. Two more are to be added soon.

Notwithstanding the good response its first centre got, adding more centres and increasing the student base has not been a cakewalk. There have been problems along the way. The market for dance being fragmented, Center Stage faces competition from a number of small-time players. These smaller institutes hold classes even in community centres and club houses of large housing colonies. They are held by individual dance instructors. Many of these classes/institutes close down before long and the students are therefore left in the lurch.

Against this backdrop, Avik and Girish are confident that they offer a far superior value proposition through Center Stage and that the market will realize this sooner than later.

Apart from the founding partners, the core team at Center Stage includes Mitali Kulkarni, Yash Lohiya, Pratima Thorat, Rekha Upadhyaya, Diparna Aeram, Avinash Shirsath and Tejas Garbhe. All of them are experienced dancers. At the same time, they have the bandwidth to think about other aspects of business too. Most importantly, all of them are on the same wavelength. This means that they appreciate the vision with which Center Stage has been launched and are pulling their weight to make the vision come true.

Center Stage has collaborated with fifteen corporate houses, twelve colleges, nine schools and pre-schools, eight well-known gymnasia and eight residential complexes in Pune — a commendable achievement in a short span of two years. The tireless efforts of the team in building Center Stage has been covered in the media too.

Avik wants to build Center Stage as an academy of performing arts. Recently, he and his team made their first foray into theatre. In future, they will probably add other art forms to their portfolio. But for now they are focused on consolidating dance and theatre.

Center Stage has now crossed the incubation phase and its operations have begun stabilizing. Soon it will be incorporated as a private limited company and a board of directors will be formed at that stage. Having a board will help the company develop its strategy and run Center Stage in a more professional manner. In the near future, a few trusted advisors are also likely to be brought on board to guide the company.

In the long run, Avik wants to enter the fitness business. He is not sure about what exactly he will do in that domain, but he has some ideas. Fitness would be a logical extension of his current business offering since dance itself is a very effective form of fitness training.

For now he is happy with the way Center Stage is shaping up. He is convinced that he and his teammates are creating a centre of excellence in performing arts, one that will be known for its deep love for all art forms, especially dance.

For Avik, dance has always been a way of life, a philosophy that has guided and enriched Avik's life all these years. He wants to make sure that it guides and enriches the lives of many others too.

Sidelights

- Avik's credo in life is – 'Others breathe to live. To me, dancing itself is like breathing.'
- He has been performing on stage since the age of three-and-a-half.

Avik's Message to Young Entrepreneurs

- I believe that creating jobs for others is better than getting into one. I have therefore always wanted to be an entrepreneur.
- People say that the lack of a good idea stops them from becoming entrepreneurs. I say that it is actually the fear of failure which holds them back. My friends, fear is a state of mind. Overcome the fear, have patience, research well, take calculated risks and you will be setting up a company instead of working in one. Always remember, 'when your passion becomes your profession, your workstation becomes your playground.' If you are a college student interested in becoming an entrepreneur, speak to your professors about it. They are sure to help you, just like my professors at Indira School of Business Studies did.

Key Learnings from Avik's Story

- Do what you love – you will find the right path though there will be obstacles. Your passion and joy in what you are doing will rub off on others; they too will start to believe in your vision and your capability.
- Even if you are working for somebody else in your area of passion, go the extra mile to improve things. Avik could have just accepted the way things were at Mrudang and Naach. But he did not do so. He tried to

make them better even though these companies were not his. This is the hallmark of a true entrepreneur.
- As an entrepreneur, you have to drive business development yourself – if you cannot sell your own ideas, who will?

10. H.H. High School
Brambe

Founder: S. Shadab Hassan
Nature of the venture: A school for rural children from poor families.
Founded in: 2010
Based in: Brambe, Jharkhand
Team size: Twenty (This includes teaching and non-teaching staff members)
Vision for the venture: To use education as an instrument for social change and help it reach the last child. The school wishes to give children in rural India a life they all deserve.
URL: www.facebook.com/hhhighschool

Take a small village twenty kilometres out side of Ranchi. Add a few hundred children from extremely poor families. Throw in a graduate from BIT Mesra. Mix this well with a supportive family and enthusiastic young volunteers. Sprinkle generous doses of vision, passion and dedication. Now shake the mixture vigorously. Voila! Your cocktail is ready. Garnish this with some technology and serve with love.

And that, in a nutshell, is the story of H.H. High School which has been serving knowledge with great love to the children of Brambe, an obscure village near Ranchi in the state of Jharkhand. It is a school that has radically transformed the lives of several hundred children and has given them a real shot at a better life.

Set deep in the hinterland of the economically backward state of Jharkhand, H.H. High School is a powerful beacon of light that is trying to banish the darkness of illiteracy. The school is proof of the power of Shadab Hassan's vision, dedication and perseverance. It is proof that anybody can make a lot of difference to a community.

In its five years of existence, the school has come a long, long way. To the villagers of Brambe, it has become a powerful symbol of hope and possibility.

THE RAINMAKER

I reach H.H. High School on a Saturday morning in November. The winter sun shines weakly on a few hundred students who have gathered for the assembly. A small group of teachers is standing on one side, watching the proceedings. I move closer to them and watch from the sidelines.

A teacher tells me that prayers for the day have just been said. Now one of the teachers, a bespectacled young man in his early twenties, is throwing questions at the students — What is the capital of Italy? What does the large intestine do? Why does a star shine? As soon as each question is shouted out, several hands go up. The young man points to different children and gives them all a chance to answer. Some answer wrong, some right. The young man handles the session deftly, his sense of comfort with the students evident. Now and then, he exhorts the children to think before they answer. After a few such questions, the assembly winds up and the children file back to their classrooms in an orderly fashion.

As the students disperse, I spend a few minutes talking to the teachers. Most of them seem to be in their late twenties or early thirties. As we talk, I notice their bright smiles, their clear eyes and their heartfelt words. Shadab Hassan, co-founder of the school and one of the prime movers behind it, shows me around the campus. I take in the trees (plenty of them!), the bicycles parked in rows and the classrooms along one side. There is a sense of peace here.

Shadab talks of how he was inspired by his father's life story to start this school. Shadab's father, Mr Shahid Hassan, had a very difficult childhood. With no money in the family, he struggled to pursue his education. Still he did not give up hope. Squaring his jaw, he sold balloons and candies in Brambe to fund his way through school and college. His mother sold a pair of gold earrings to help him fill out his Matriculation form. His maternal uncle sold his gold ring to help him fill up the intermediate form. Over a period of time, Mr Hassan became a professor of psychology at Ranchi University.

Aware of his father's struggles, Shadab was clear that he would go back to his village after graduation and help his father set up a school there so that other poor children did not have to struggle the way his father did. An MBA from BIT Mesra, he rejected attractive job offers from Tata Teleservices and Vodafone and chose instead to return to his village.

At first, he thought he would work in a corporate for five years, save some money and then set up the school. But he realized if he did that, the children of the village would lose another five years of their lives. He discussed the matter with his parents and they all decided to set the school up immediately. He did this in spite of the fact that theirs was a middle-class family with limited savings. They didn't have the money, infrastructure or connections necessary to run a school. What they did have though was a burning desire to give the poor children of their village a good education which would, in turn, give them a better life.

Shadab, his mother and a couple of friends went around Brambe informing villagers about the new school. They urged parents to send their children to attend. A few agreed, while most did not. Finally, on 16 January 2010, H.H. High School opened its doors. On that first day, it had eighty children on its rolls, spread over nursery to Class 8 along with six teachers. Shadab's mother Mrs Roshan Ara was named the principal. It was an intensely proud moment for everyone, especially Shadab's father.

At that time, money was a big constraint (it still is, though to a lesser extent). The family did not possess the necessary funds to build proper infrastructure for the school. But that didn't deter them. Shadab's dad had bought a small plot of land in Brambe many years ago and had planted several trees on it. He had also been constructing a house little by little over a period of time. The family decided to run the school from this small, half-constructed house. At that time, the house was just a shell – no doors, no tiling, no electricity ... nothing.

For the first few weeks, the children attended their classes sitting on durries (woven carpets) that had been hired from tent houses (the ones supplied to weddings and other functions) for Rs 20 per day. The school hired four of them. It didn't even have the money to buy the durries since each cost Rs 600.

It was after a fortnight that Shadab managed to get a few second-hand wooden benches from a school in the city that had shut down a few weeks ago. At least some of the children now had benches to sit on.

The room that was supposed to be the kitchen was turned into a classroom. So were other parts of the house. Since there was no money to buy blackboards, they used the roll-up kind. The entire school had to manage with three of these boards. When one class did not need a board, it was simply rolled up and taken to another.

Shadab and his team decided to keep the fees very low, given how poor most of the people in the area were. They decided to charge just Rs 100 per child per month. And yet the school had just eighty students. That brings us to the other big problem Shadab faced (and continues to face), which is the entrenched mindset of the villagers. Most of them do not think about education at all. In a tradition handed down from one generation to the next, many rural Indian children are simply sent out to work in the field or a shop, or are made to help with household chores.

This is the harsh reality in most of our villages, especially in east and north India. It is true that many parents do this because they are extremely poor and don't have the money to send their kids to school. But at the same time, many other parents *do* have the money and yet don't care to educate their children. This is because education is simply not a priority for them.

In order to fight this mindset, Shadab and his small team started a campaign called 'Reach2teach'. They went around Brambe and other neighbouring villages, meeting villagers and explaining why they should send their children to a good school. They wanted to help parents realize the difference between 'going to school' and 'learning in school'. They explained to the parents that education could improve their lives drastically. Apart from helping their children get good jobs, it would also mould them into good human beings.

This campaign worked wonders. Several more parents started sending their children to H.H. High School. A sudden increase in the number of students meant that there was now a shortage of teachers! But this was a happy problem for the team – it was better than not having any children in the school! It was time now to roll out another campaign – this time to find more good teachers. Seeing that it was difficult to find qualified teachers in the area who were willing to teach for a low salary, Shadab and his team thought of an unconventional method to find them – they tapped the colleges in towns nearby and requested students to come and teach at their school. They named this campaign 'Volunteer2teach'. Different subjects were allotted to different college students. Those from BIT Mesra, IIM Ranchi, IIT Kharagpur, St Xavier's Ranchi and Central University of Jharkhand responded with great enthusiasm. On weekends and other holidays, they would come to Brambe and teach science, English, maths, etc. But more than just teaching the subjects, they also opened the eyes of the children to the world outside – they spoke about their own fields of study, the kind of careers and dreams they were chasing, life in the city along and so many other things.

On Independence Day 2011, the school started another unique tradition, something it follows even today. Instead of inviting well-known people as chief guests for the Independence Day and Republic Day celebrations, the school gave this honour to people who were helping the school in its cause. So if it was Sajjad Ansari on one occasion, it was Khadija Didi on another. In the early days of the school, Sajjad bhai had ferried children from home to school and back in an autorickshaw, completely free of charge. Since children did not have any other means of conveyance, this played a big role in getting more parents to send their children to school. Khadija Didi on the other hand is a cleaner and caretaker at the school. While this might be viewed as a menial job in most schools, in H.H. High School it is a job of great importance. Everybody sees Khadija Didi as one of the custodians of the school, someone who keeps things in order and the premises clean. This makes a big difference to the lives of children inside the campus.

Says Shadab, 'To us, these are the real freedom heroes. We think it is just right that these people, rather than local big shots, hoist our flag.'

About a year after he launched the school, Shadab experienced one of the biggest moments in his life. At a seminar hosted by the Central University of Jharkhand, he met that most ardent of champions of India's youth – Dr A.P.J. Abdul Kalam. When people in the audience were given the chance to ask Dr Kalam questions, Shadab asked one too. After telling Dr Kalam about his school, he asked him the three things he would do if he had been running H.H. High School instead. In his characteristic style, Dr Kalam said that he would 1) plant as many trees as possible in the school campus; 2) try to enrol as many children and 3) invite eminent people from all walks of life to interact with the children.

With a swollen chest, Shadab informed Dr Kalam that they were already doing two of the three things and would soon start acting on the third suggestion too. At that time, the school campus had 1500 trees and saplings. And the number of children studying there had gone up from 80 to 250 in a single academic year. Dr Kalam wished him all the best and told him that he was doing something noble, something India needed very much.

Almost a year later, Shadab was awarded the Yuva Prabodhan, 2012 award by Dr Kalam during the launch of the 'What Can I Give' mission in Jharkhand.

Shadab's effort has to be seen in the right perspective to understand its magnitude fully. Economically, Jharkhand has always lagged behind most other states of India. And Brambe is one of its poorer parts. As mentioned earlier, most adults have neither the money nor the desire to send their children to school. In this context, you need enormous will power and perseverance to convince such parents that school education is important for their children. During their 'Reach2teach' campaign (which is conducted every year to enrol more students), Shadab and team focus on the transformational power of education – the fact that it can completely change a child's life by helping him or her build a solid career. For most parents, this is the clincher.

But the problem is greater than just getting children to join the school. These are kids who have not seen a book in their lives. Most of them have no idea what mathematics, science, English, history, etc. is. So how does one even start teaching them? Many of the children may have gone to other schools in the past, but learnt practically nothing.

In the beginning, this problem was acute enough to give Shadab and his small team nightmares. The teachers had to teach the children using lots of pictures and the simplest of Hindi words. Also, many children were admitted two levels lower! For instance, those who had studied till Class 3 in another school were taken into Class 1 at H.H. High School.

Progress was painfully slow at first. Over the next few years, the school slowly accelerated the rate of learning and managed to bring the children on an even keel. But even today, everything is taught using very simple Hindi words and a lot of repetition. Wondrously, this does not sap the teachers' energy at all. They continue with the same verve. As a result of this constant grooming, kids in the higher classes are now able to understand English.

Shadab is understandably pained that many villagers do not send their children to school even though they can afford it. 'We charge just Rs 150 per month for the lower classes and Rs 200 per month for the higher classes. This is less than what people spend on tea! Yet it is a struggle to convince them.'

Imagine the joy therefore, when he meets someone like Salomi Tigga. A grandmother of seven children, she has been single-handedly ensuring that all of them go to H.H. High School. This, despite facing stiff opposition from her own son and daughter (the son is the father of three of those children while the daughter is the mother of the remaining four). Salomi sells *hadiya,* the local arrack. Every month, she saves some money from her meagre earnings in order to pay the fees for the children. Seeing her plight, Shadab and his mother decided to educate three of these seven children free. Salomi pays a small amount for the other four.

People like Salomi are an important part of this movement for change that Shadab and his family have started. Recognizing this, the school made Salomi the chief guest at the Independence Day celebrations last year.

Though running an educational institution under these circumstances is in itself a great thing, Shadab is keen to ensure that this is not just any school, but a truly great one. After all, a school named after his grandfather Mr Hamid Hassan, who was a freedom fighter, can't be just another school! It is a matter of obsession with Shadab that the children are taught in a manner that makes them not just ready for life, but also ready as future contributors to the well-being of our country.

This explains why the school takes a truly multi-dimensional approach to learning. The curriculum goes far beyond textbooks. It lays a lot of emphasis on practical learning and an all-round exposure to life on a larger scale. For instance, children are urged to find new ways of reusing materials. This reduces waste and the burden on the environment to some extent. Christmas of 2011 will always be a memorable one for the whole school because this was the first festival they celebrated in a fully eco-friendly manner. Students made lamps, a Christmas tree and other decorative items using discarded bottle caps, empty bottles, fused light bulbs, etc. They also made Christmas caps for themselves using chart paper.

And then there is the 'Live Classroom' concept. Realizing that it was impossible for volunteers to come to the school every day to teach as they had exams and other priorities too, Shadab decided to leverage technology so that anybody who wants to teach can do so from wherever they are. The school uses Skype and Google Hangout to organize live interactions with people from all walks of life. In an emotional moment, Shadab's mother kicked off this concept in February 2012. She was then in the USA, staying with Shadab's sister. She addressed the entire school over Skype from there. Soon after that, Shadab's brother-in-law, an engineer at Intel, came online and explained to the children all about Intel and what the company does. Another time an oil engineer from Kuwait showed the kids the whole process of drilling and extracting oil! A team from Google, Bengaluru followed suit. These sessions continue even today, with several people volunteering to teach the children something or the other.

No wonder these sessions send Brambe's kids into raptures! Come to think of it, even children living in cities do not get this kind of exposure.

In stark contrast to the attitude of the parents is that of the children. From the first day, they have been lapping up all that the school has to offer. They remind me of many thirsty kittens drinking from a large bowl of milk. They participate in every activity – a Bikathon in Ranchi, a clean-up drive in the village, extra classes conducted after regular hours, sports day celebrations, etc. – like there is no tomorrow.

Considering their background and upbringing, the children have come a long way in academics too. The first batch of Class 10 graduated from the school in 2012. The entire class of sixteen students passed the board exams, with the topper scoring 77 per cent marks. The subsequent batches have performed equally well. Students in younger classes do well too. Most of them are now comfortable with the basic use of a computer and have learnt the use of MS Office. When a team from IIT Kharagpur landed up at the school to conduct a workshop on robotics, they were astounded by the speed with which the children learnt things. As part of the workshop, the children were asked to help the visitors build remote-controlled cars. With the active participation of the children, the team assembled thirty-five cars in just ninety minutes!

Faced with such a response, the entire team at the school is keen to keep improving and doing more for the children. Shadab constantly keeps looking at what other schools are doing so that he can adopt their best practices. But he and his team go much further than that – they spend hours reading up on the internet and having intense discussions amongst themselves on how they can keep improving their school. Most of the ideas and initiatives they have implemented so far have come from within – from a realization that if education is delivered the right way, it can transform an individual for the better.

In his attempt to create this ecosystem, Shadab has received help from a number of people and organizations. Some of them, like his friend Abhishek Kumar, have been with him right from the beginning. Others have joined along the way, seeing the power of his dream. Like Kumar

Saurabh who keeps the momentum going by constantly engaging the kids in one activity after another. His wife Neha has also been by his side all along, constantly working for the school and giving Shadab the much needed emotional support on this tough journey. She has actively partnered Shadab in all the campaigns they have run for the school so far.

Facebook has helped Shadab enormously in his search for the right set of volunteers and like-minded associates. Early on, Shadab opened a Facebook page for his school. Ever since, he has been using it to spread the word about the school and to enlist help whenever required. And help has literally poured in through different forms. Several people have donated money, books, skills and time to the school. Even organizations have come forth to do their bit. Since most children of the school did not have proper sweaters, books, pencil boxes, shoes, etc., Shadab reached out to Goonj for help. Run by Anshu Gupta, Goonj is an NGO based in Delhi which helps poor and homeless people. Among other initiatives, Goonj distributes blankets and warm clothing to the needy before the onset of the harsh winter every year.

Goonj responded promptly, putting together a truckload of things for the school. And when Shadab found that he did not have the money to transport the stuff to Brambe, he reached out to people using Facebook again. And yet again, they responded. Even unknown people chipped in, contributing whatever amount they could. It took Shadab two months to crowdsource the necessary funds and bring the truck full of things from Delhi to Brambe. 'But the delight on the children's faces made all this effort worthwhile. We undertake all these campaigns and initiatives only so that the children can focus on learning without worrying about books, stationery, shoes, etc.'

Shadab is immensely grateful to all those who have contributed to his effort in one way or another.

In January 2015, H.H. High School turned five. It has come a long way in the five years. Having overcome the initial challenges, the focus now is on improving its financial systems so that Shadab can utilize money better. The school is set to break-even this year. From the next year, whatever profits the school makes will be ploughed back into it — to improve the infrastructure and the quality of education.

Shadab knows it is vital to run the school as a profit-making venture while at the same time not losing sight of its vision for societal improvement. He is keen to ensure that every rupee coming into the school be used in the best possible manner. Among other things, he wants to start a system through which donors are kept informed of the progress of the school and about how their money is being spent.

Shadab's journey has been an extremely emotional one, with several ups and downs. Helping children learn, giving them knowledge and exposure of life and the world is indeed a noble thing to do. Still, he and his team have not let the nobility of their work go to their heads (you'd be surprised at how many people have let this happen). They remain as humble as they were five years ago and continue to do their good work with great focus, dedication and resourcefulness. Shadab and his family want to add Classes 11 and 12 to the school soon and a little later, set up a college too.

India needs many more Shadabs. I'm sure they are waiting in the wings. Who knows, they could be reading this book! Heck, it could even be you!

Sidelights

- Shadab loves to drive. He says he can drive twenty-four hours a day. While most of us feel tired after some time behind the wheel, Shadab feels tired and stressed if he sits in the passenger seat for too long!

Shadab's Message to Young Entrepreneurs

- Do what you can with what you have, wherever you are. At H.H. High School, this is what we are doing. Many people have the intent; some of them have the resources too. But they keep waiting for the 'right time' or 'right opportunity' to begin. Ultimately, they end up not doing what they wanted to.
- No idea is great by itself. The intent and perseverance with which you take it forward is what makes it great. So it doesn't matter how big or small your start is. If it makes a positive change in someone's life, directly or indirectly, do it!

Key Lessons from Shadab's Story

- If a lofty vision is backed by a steely will, you can even move mountains. It is only because of his strong will (not to mention the support of his family and team, of course) that Shadab has been able to fight several odds and nurture the school over the past five years.
- When you need help in anything, just reach out to as many people as you can. And someone will *surely* respond.
- Even if your venture/institution is addressing a societal problem, like Shadab's school is, make sure it is world-class and profitable. Do not stop pursuing excellence in what you do and what you offer to the market.

11. Nurturing Green
Delhi

Founder: Annu Grover
Name of the company: Nurturing Green
Brand name: Nurturing Green
Nature of business: Sale of plants for gifting and for the decoration of homes and commercial spaces.
Founded in: 2010
Based in: Delhi
Team size: Sixty
Vision for the business: To put a plant in every hand that goes out to gift! To nurture anything that is green.
URL: www.nurturinggreen.in

Like so many of us, Annu never thought he'd be an entrepreneur. He fits the classic stereotype of the urban yuppie – studied management in college, went abroad to pursue higher studies and then joined a firm there. However, he quit this job and returned to India soon to be close to his family. It was only then that his tryst with entrepreneurship began.

Initially, Annu took some impulsive and possibly naïve decisions which backfired on him. Still, he did not lose heart. He learnt valuable lessons every step of the way. Finally, he set up Nurturing Green and since then has managed to make it a fast-growing and profitable company.

More than anything else, Annu's is a story of twists and turns. And of grit, perseverance and resilience.

SHOOTS OF JOY

We meet at the Nurturing Green retail outlet in Greater Kailash in Delhi. Annu has given me precise directions as a result of which I find the outlet easily. The humidity of the September morning is high enough to sap my energy in the two minutes I spend gazing at the storefront from across the road. I hurry across, seeking respite from the heat and humidity.

Inside the store it is cool, thanks to the plants that take up most of the space. There are different kinds of plants all around me, some big, others small. Just beyond the store, I can catch glimpses of a greenhouse. Annu Grover walks in a few minutes later and apologizes for being late. He shows me around the store and the greenhouse and introduces me to his staff.

Until mid-2009, Annu never imagined he would run his own company someday. Growing up, he wanted the things any regular guy would want – a good job, a successful career and a good lifestyle. With this in mind, he joined the MBA programme at BIMTECH, Noida. After he graduated in 2009, he got an offer for the post of management trainee in a company called Guardian Pharmacy, which runs a chain of medical stores, for a monthly salary of Rs 25,000.

But before he could join the company as an intern, he got a chance to attend a nine-month programme in Austria called Global Business Programme. He won a scholarship for the programme which was run by the F.H. Joanneum University of Applied Sciences. The scholarship covered the programme fee and travel expenses. He was also given an allowance of 1000 Euros a month, which Annu found out was enough to live on.

Life in the city of Graz in Austria was very different from that in Delhi. Annu's class was multi-ethnic; it had students from all over the world. Spending time with them gave Annu a wider perspective on life and the world. He understood the views, outlooks and life priorities of his classmates from different nations. 'It opened my eyes. Until then, I hadn't imagined that people from different cultures could look at life and things in so many different ways. Even the way some of them looked at a problem and tried to solve it was different from my way!' says Annu, his sense of wonder showing in his eyes.

It was in Austria that he got the idea for his life-changing business. On his birthday in 2009, several classmates gave him gifts. One of them was a small, beautiful potted plant given to him by Miroslav, his friend from Croatia.

Miroslav told him that this was not some ordinary plant but that it had a certain significance. He told Annu that the croton is supposed to be the plant that corresponds to the zodiac sign Leo (Annu's zodiac sign). Annu learnt that all twelve zodiac signs have a corresponding plant and was touched at getting such a refreshingly different gift. He turned to Google to learn more about this. As he read up on this subject, he kept thinking that it would be a great idea to gift plants to people on important occasions. He thought people would be pleasantly surprised to receive a plant as a gift as against conventional gifts like a pen, a watch, a gadget, clothes, bouquets, etc. Also, plants have lasting value because they can keep growing and beautifying one's home as long as one waters them regularly. There was a third advantage in gifting plants. The person who receives the plant comes that much closer to nature because once he gets a plant as a gift, he would want to nurture it. He would not feel like throwing it away.

Annu felt this idea would work in India, which has a strong culture of gifting. Be it a festival, an anniversary or a birthday, people visit family and friends carrying a lot of gifts. They'd love to add a nice little plant to their set of gifts. Also, with cities getting increasingly polluted, Annu thought there was a good reason to urge people to gift plants.

Annu's belief in the power of this idea was strengthened a month later. On his parents' wedding anniversary Annu arranged to have a bouquet of flowers delivered to his parents on the special day. Some time later, he called up to wish them. Speaking to his mother, he asked her if she liked the bouquet. She said yes, she and his dad loved it. However, since the flowers had started wilting a short while later, they had thrown the bouquet away.

A disappointed Annu was left thinking that he should have sent his parents a plant instead.

Anyway, life went on. Annu finished the nine-month management programme and joined a company called Maya India E.U. as a consultant. His role was to help foreign companies set up shop in India. He had to help them understand the legal and socio-cultural issues involved in doing business in India. In other words, help them acclimatize to the Indian way of living, working and doing business so that the company could get off to a good start in India. Doing business in a foreign country can be tough for any company since it has to understand the way the country's people, systems and government work. Some assistance in navigating these waters would therefore be of great help to a company seeking to set up operations on foreign shores.

Initially Annu liked the job. It was his first one and wasn't very tough (since he had an extensive network of contacts in India which proved handy for this role). Besides, the pay was good. But in a few months, he started feeling restless. He wanted to do something on his own and not work for somebody else. Also, the urge to come back to India and do something meaningful had taken root in his mind.

I ask him why he got this urge. Annu is not sure of the reason. He hasn't sat back and analysed it. All he knows is that deep in his heart, he must have felt the need to give something back to society in return for the excellent upbringing and education he has enjoyed. 'My parents brought me up with excellent values. In doing so, they must have passed on the thought that I should not just make money, but also do something for others in the bargain,' is how he sums it up.

Still, he didn't want to take a rash decision and leave his job. He therefore requested the management of his company to transfer him to Delhi so that he could kill *three* birds with one stone. He could continue to do his job from Delhi – probably more effectively since it was all about helping companies set up businesses in India. At the same time, he would be close to his family. The third thing was that he could start doing some groundwork for setting up his own venture. His company agreed and transferred him to Delhi. But even after coming back, Annu continued to be dissatisfied. There was nothing wrong with the job or the company; it was just that his heart was not in it. He was itching to get out and experience the sense of liberation that comes with doing something on your own.

And so, one day in May 2009, he quit the company and set up an organization called Empowerment of Youth for Environment Conservation (EYEC). Through EYEC, Annu wanted to make people more sensitive to issues related to the environment and urban ecology. He had noticed that most people were indifferent to these issues which thereby led to the steady destruction of our urban ecology year after year. Thoughtless disposal of waste, the depleting green cover of our cities and the rising levels of pollution were just a few of the issues that concerned Annu. He wanted EYEC to highlight the benefits of being more responsible towards our environment, thus sparking a change in the behaviour of people.

One of the initiatives EYEC ran was called Tree Huggers. The objective was to make the city of Delhi carbon-neutral, that is, to compensate for the carbon dioxide emitted as a result of day-to-day activities like using an air-conditioner, travelling by car, bus or motorcycle, etc. This emission of carbon dioxide into the atmosphere in turn leads to global warming. The quantum of emissions can be calculated. The idea behind Tree Huggers was to calculate the carbon emissions of individuals/organizations and then offset these emissions by planting the required number of trees as trees release oxygen into the air and neutralize the emission of carbon dioxide.

Annu and his team at EYEC approached a few companies with the idea of helping them become carbon neutral. They told the companies that they would calculate the quantum of carbon dioxide released by the offices of the company and then plant the requisite number of trees somewhere in Delhi or its vicinity. In return for this effort, EYEC asked to be paid a certain sum of money. This money would cover EYEC's costs (such as printing leaflets and brochures, hiring people to plant the trees, finding suitable land where they could be planted, conveyance expenses, etc.) and leave a small profit for the team.

Annu thought companies would be happy to participate in such an initiative because it would give them good publicity. Such an initiative would fit within their agenda for Corporate Social Responsibility (CSR). Much to his disappointment however, he found that the companies EYEC approached were not willing to pay for this initiative. Some of them even offered to give EYEC the necessary resources (like people and materials) for planting trees but none of them was willing to pay money for it.

The team tried implementing a few other projects, some of which were meant to help poor people. For instance, they collected excess food from Annu's alma mater BIMTECH and gave it to needy people. However, a few months after trying his hand at such projects, he realized that it was very difficult to make money this way. It was hard to convince organizations to shell out money for CSR initiatives. Annu found that the companies he met wanted the mileage that came from such initiatives, but were reluctant to pay for that mileage. Day-to-day sustenance had become difficult for the EYEC team. Also, Annu had to repay the education loan he had taken when he joined BIMTECH.

After thinking long and hard about the situation, Annu took the emotional decision of putting EYEC on the back burner. This was in January 2010. While his heart rebelled against this decision, his head told him that this was the only sensible way forward for him. He knew that through EYEC, he had tried to do something good, something noble. But it was not sustainable as it was not profitable.

There was no point trying to feed someone else if one remained hungry oneself.

And so, it was time to decide what he would do next.

Not surprisingly, his mind went back to the idea of making a business out of gifting plants. He thought that this idea was the ideal combination of a good cause and a commercial business model. Already many months had passed since he first thought of this idea. He did not want to lose any more time. And so without further ado, he started working out the business model.

Since the purpose behind this venture was to make people gift plants, Annu wondered if he could offer them free of cost to the person who wanted to gift it. The way he saw it, if someone wanted to gift their friend a plant, all they had to do was call up Annu and request the plant be delivered to their friend's doorstep. Annu would not charge the caller for the plant. Instead, he would approach companies and offer them the opportunity to place their branding on the pots for a sum of money. That way the venture would earn revenue. For a company, placing its logo and tagline on the pot would be a good way of earning mileage for its brand. Annu thought companies would be willing to pay for this opportunity and include the cost in their marketing budget.

He approached many companies with this proposal. Most turned him down because they were not convinced that it would work.

Finally he managed to sell the idea to the State Bank of India, which agreed to give it a try. The bank decided to buy 200 plants with their branding on the pots and gift these to prospective customers in a place where they were going to open a branch soon. Unfortunately, the bank backed out at the last minute saying it was not a feasible idea.

Annu felt a worm of unease. He realized that his revenue model was not feasible because of a few inherent problems. For one, in this age of high-power (and increasingly digital) advertising messages, a branded pot would not be a great communication medium. Like Annu had already found out by then, it was very difficult to convince brands to put money on this advertising route. Secondly, it is always dangerous to offer anything for free to someone in India. The dominant Indian mentality is to pile on the freebies. So there was a good chance that demand for these free potted plants would skyrocket every now and then, leaving Annu gasping in an attempt to keep up. With his tiny team and very limited financial resources, there was no way he could cater to the huge demand.

After spending several anxious days trying to find a way out, Annu decided to simplify his business model. He decided to try selling the plants to people. In other words, people could buy potted plants from him for a price (whether to keep them for themselves or gift them). He knew that several people keep plants at home for decorative purposes. Many of them live in independent houses/bungalows or spacious apartments – you'll find many such houses in central Delhi even today – and love to keep plants. These houses have the necessary space to accomodate a few plants, either in the form of a balcony, a small terrace or a courtyard. Extending this logic a little further, Annu thought that even commercial organizations like restaurants, clubs and offices would want to buy plants to decorate their premises. It looked like there was a market for such an idea.

In January 2010, Annu decided to explore this opportunity. He decided to name his new venture 'Nurturing Green' and get it incorporated as a company. He thought this name would give him latitude to get into any business associated with the environment and the word 'green'. So he could start with plants today and later on move into landscaping, farming and even horticulture.

Annu recounts these events in a slightly philosophical manner. His tone becomes sombre now and then and his eyes are a window to the uncertainty and apprehension he must have felt during those tough times. I share this observation of mine with him and he nods his head in agreement. 'Yeah, that was a turbulent phase. I made a few big mistakes and lost my way. But I also learnt a lot from that experience.'

He adds that, during these testing times, it would have been easiest for him to join his father's business or take up a job somewhere. His father was keen that he join the family business and take it forward. But Annu did not want to do that. Having taken the entrepreneurial plunge, he wanted to give it his best shot. He wanted to do something substantial on his own. 'My family and friends told me it was foolish to quit a good job and potter about with plants. But I didn't want to give up without a strong fight,' he says with a grin. And so he kept up his quest for the right business idea and for success.

'You must have felt very lonely during that phase,' I suggest. He says yes, he did. However, his girlfriend (who is now his wife) stood by him every step of the way. She listened to his troubles patiently, empathized with him and gave him the firm emotional support he needed to keep moving ahead. During the lean months, she even paid Annu's bills from her salary. Her support for him and his efforts has been unstinting and complete throughout.

Nurturing Green started full-fledged operations in April 2010. Mayank Gupta, one of Annu's childhood friends joined him to help set it up. There were a hundred things to be done and only the two of them to do them. It was strenuous yet exciting. Annu started tapping into his network of contacts in Delhi to create business for his company. Through one of these contacts, he met the secretary of the Noida Golf Course. The gentleman must have been impressed by the zeal displayed by the youngster sitting in front of him because he immediately ordered a few plants from Nurturing Green for the golf course. He did not even ask to see the plants. After this, other orders came in, most of them small-sized ones. The profit per order was very low. Annu kept making sales calls, mainly to educational institutions and companies. But convincing people proved to be tougher than he had imagined. There were times when the company did not bag a single order for weeks! For the rest of that year, Nurturing Green just plodded along. Annu remembers 2010 as being a year of terrible uncertainty and anxiety.

Tired of making calls and trying to push up the sales of plants, Annu decided to open a retail outlet and try selling from there. He thought it might help to have a standing presence at a prominent location like a mall so that people visiting the place would notice his brand. That way, word about Nurturing Green might spread faster. He approached the owner of Shipra Mall in Indirapuram in Ghaziabad and explained his situation to him. He requested the owner to give him some space in the mall so that he could put up his store. The owner took pity on Annu and gave him a small area in the forecourt just outside the mall. What's more, he did not charge rent for this space. He told Annu he could take the space for six months on a trial basis and stock his plants there.

To Annu, it was manna from heaven! 'This was the first good thing that had happened to me in more than a year! I was speechless.' And so Nurturing Green's first store came up at Shipra Mall. Annu hired a sales executive and a gardener to help him run the show. The executive would make sales calls while Annu manned the store. Sitting in the forecourt of the mall, Annu's tiny store did not have the comfort of air-conditioning. He therefore had to brave the elements. He recalls sitting there all day, through the harsh summer and stinging rain.

While waiting for customers to come to his store, Annu started developing a proper product portfolio for the company – that is, a range of plants the company could offer. He knew that having a range of popular plants that catered to different tastes would be very important for the success of his venture. This was also the time when he started developing his network of plant suppliers. One day, he found out that some poor, uneducated women in Kolkata were making jute pots for plants. He immediately reached out to these women through someone who knew them. He discovered that the pots were of excellent quality and agreed to buy a certain number of jute pots from them. Back in Delhi, he sold these pots (with plants) to a few companies. The companies were very happy to buy them since the pots were made from a natural fibre and looked very elegant. 'I am really happy I struck a deal with those women. They were making very good pots. By buying from them, I was able to help them in a small way. At the same time, it made business sense for my company.'

In May 2011, Annu participated in the Power of Ideas (POI) competition conducted by the *Economic Times*. Thanks to this, Nurturing Green received some exposure in the media over the next few months. The company emerged as one of the twenty-five best start-ups in the competition. Annu had the rare honour of receiving his certificate and cheque from Mr Narayana Murthy, one of the founders of Infosys. The cheque was for an amount of Rs 5 lakh and was a grant from the Department of Science and Technology of the Government of India. As luck would have it, a picture of Annu receiving this award from Narayana Murthy appeared in the *Economic Times* the next morning. This led to a flurry of calls and interviews with journalists, attracting more publicity for the company. 'That was a heady time. After the pain and struggles of the earlier eighteen months, this was really unexpected! I didn't know what to think or say,' says Annu.

Thanks to all the publicity, Annu started receiving calls from more and more people who wanted to buy his potted plants. His order inflow grew. For Annu though, the real gain from all this mileage was not the inflow of orders, but the fact that his father finally accepted his son was indeed doing something good. He called Annu up and spoke to him at length. This again was an emotionally charged moment because his father was speaking to him after a long interval.

Participating in POI brought the company a windfall too. An investment firm based in Dubai saw the POI event film that had been uploaded on YouTube and found the idea of Nurturing Green very interesting. They contacted Annu and said that they would like to invest in his company. A stunned Annu didn't know how to react. He asked for some time to think about the offer. Mulling it over, Annu realized that his company could grow much faster if they had some extra cash in hand. The money could be invested into the business – setting up more stores, hiring competent people, maintaining a larger inventory of plants, buying higher-priced plants, etc. He decided to tell the investment firm that he was interested in the deal. Over the next month, the firm invested a reasonably large sum of money into Nurturing Green.

Finally, finally, it looked like Nurturing Green had turned the corner. For the first time in his entrepreneurial journey, Annu felt that he and his company were on a strong wicket. They had a strong business idea and were now ready to back it up with robust execution.

So far, Annu had been lurching ahead; it was now time to start sprinting.

Another shift of gears happened soon when Annu and his team realized that gifting was a small segment in the market for plants. The decor segment was a much bigger and more profitable slice of this market. It included two sub-segments – home decor and commercial space decor. The team decided to initially enter the home decor sub-segment. They approached Lifestyle (a chain of department stores) with a proposal to open a shop-in-shop in Home Centre, the brand under which Lifestyle sells furniture, furnishing and everything else pertaining to home decor. The logic behind the proposal was simple. People who come to Home Centre are looking to furnish and decorate their homes. It therefore made sense to also offer plants under the same roof. After buying a cot, a dining table and some curtains, a customer is very likely to consider buying plants if he/she were to see them in the same store.

Annu and his team convinced Lifestyle of the merit of the idea and signed a deal to open a fifty square foot shop-in-shop in the Home Centre outlet at The Great India Place, a mall in Noida. The shop-in-shop was a success from the word go. It has been clocking a sizeable revenue every month. The success of this shop-in-shop led to the opening of more such outlets at other home decor stores such as @ Home, Home Stop and Home Town. All the Nurturing Green shop-in-shops have been successful so far.

At the same time, the company kept opening stand-alone retail outlets at key locations in Delhi and a few other cities. Today Nurturing Green has twenty-six retail outlets across four cities – Delhi/NCR, Bengaluru, Chennai and Jaipur. Of these, eleven are in Delhi. More such outlets will come up in other cities soon. Each store has a manager who is fully in charge of it. Depending upon the size of the business in the store, it would have one or two store sales executives helping the manager.

Since the time it opened its first store in Delhi in 2012, Nurturing Green has grown into a sixty-member organization. Annu's team is very young. The average age was in the mid-twenties. Having turned thirty now, Annu is one of the oldest in the team!

Nurturing Green is already busy hiring for its stores across India. In 2014, the company set up an e-commerce portal on its website. This enables it to cater to orders from across India. Ever since, online sales have been growing strongly month after month. Annu doesn't want to expand too fast and is instead focusing on sustainable expansion of operations.

He has also hired an HR manager to implement a proper people management policy for the organization. The HR manager helps Annu manage employees well, reward them in line with their performance and nurture them for bigger roles.

Hiring people for various roles also frees up Annu's bandwidth and helps him spend more time on strategic issues like expansion of the business, building the right culture in the company, driving cost-efficiency, etc.

Like every other entrepreneur, his company is his life's breath. In the past, he has had to stretch every fibre of his being in pursuit of sustenance and stability for Nurturing Green. But now, because the company is stable, profitable and growing, he is heaving a sigh of relief. He is able to pay his teammates good salaries and even bought himself a car recently. Most importantly, his customers are happy and are recommending Nurturing Green to others.

This long and arduous journey has taught Annu a lot about business and life. Overall, it has been a humbling experience. In addition to financial pressure and emotional stress, he has had to face his share of health problems along the way.

Today Annu has mellowed down just a bit. While his energy and passion remain undimmed, he has learnt to balance his time between family and business. Even so, he is clear that the decision to become an entrepreneur has been the best one of his life.

SIDELIGHTS

- Annu has a collection of more than 100 quotes and sayings about life, business and entrepreneurship. Whenever he feels low, he turns to them for inspiration. He says that they invariably cure him of his anxiety or disappointment.

Annu Grover's Message to Young Entrepreneurs

- My message to you, dear reader, is actually a set of three quotes I read somewhere.
- 'Choose the job you love and you will never have to work a day in your life.' – Confucius
- 'It's not always that you get to hit the iron when it is hot; believe in hitting it so hard that it *gets* hot.' – Laxmi Narayan Mittal, CEO of Arcelor-Mittal
- 'A ship is safe in harbour, but that's not what ships are built for.' – William Shedd

12. Funding Fundas

Funding. The million (or even billion) dollar question on the minds of most entrepreneurs. An issue that confuses the hell out of many since they are not sure when to raise, how to raise, how much to raise, whether to raise at all or not, and so on. If you are setting up a venture, you'd better have your fundas about funding clear.

To get you started, here are two perspectives on funding – one from an investor and the other from an entrepreneur who has raised funds. I hope this will clear many of your doubts and break some common misconceptions about funding.

For starters, let's hear Sanjay Anandaram's thoughts.

Funding – An Investor's Perspective

Sanjay has over twenty-five years of experience as a corporate professional, investor, entrepreneur and mentor to start-ups. He was a founding member of JumpStartUp Venture Fund, a pioneering early stage investing company. His recent involvement has been with companies like

FUNDING FUNDAS | 207

redBus, ShieldSquare, Ozone Media and Insta Health Solutions. Sanjay is a venture partner with Seedfund and an advisor to Ojas Ventures and KARSEM Venture Fund. He is also a prolific writer and a go-to man for many (including me, when I was writing this book!).

So, without further ado, here we go!

1. What are some of the common misconceptions related to the funding/financing of start-ups?
   Sanjay: The most common ones I have observed are:
   i) That funding is an end in itself, rather than the beginning of a long journey; ii) That investors will invest and disappear from the scene!

2. What are the key aspects of start-up funding that an entrepreneur should be aware of?
   Sanjay: Investors want to back good teams that are chasing large, fast-growing market opportunities in a differentiated manner. A good, realistic business plan that can be executed by a team is important. It would be worthwhile for entrepreneurs to understand the different legal terms associated with raising money. It is sensible to take the help of a legal advisor.

3. What is the meaning of boot strapping? Under what circumstances/in what situations is this the best way to fund a venture?
   Sanjay: Bootstrapping refers to starting up with your own funds. Or raising money from executing customer

projects and the like. In other words, no external funding. It is useful to do this if the business has to be proven before larger amounts of capital are required to be raised or if the entrepreneur wishes to retain 100 per cent freedom and control while building the business in the time and manner of his/her choosing.

4. What are the other main methods of funding that a start-up can consider? Briefly, please mention the circumstances under which each of these methods will make sense to an entrepreneur.
Sanjay: You can raise money from (i) friends and family (ii) angel investors; investors who loan relatively small amounts to entrepreneurs at a very early stage of the start-up's life (iii) venture capital funds (iv) government grants (vi) banks and (vii) customers.

If large sums of money, expertise and experience in various aspects of company building are required, then professional investors are useful. These could be angels (for up to a few crore rupees) or venture capital (for tens of crores!). If the business has to be able to demonstrate proof of traction or is in its R&D state, then bootstrapping or raising money from friends, family or the government is a good way.

Banks are useful when the business has predictable cash flows, so as to be able to service the debt. Of course, customers are always a good source of funds too! The advance you take from them can source your venture. But this is applicable only in certain kinds of businesses.

5. There is a lot of noise about the valuation of enterprises. The media is gushing about it and many entrepreneurs drool over it too. How would you advise an entrepreneur to look at enterprise valuation?
   Sanjay: Valuations are like money in the mirror – that is, an image, but not the real thing. Don't get too excited by them! Focus on building a great company and the valuation will happen as a consequence. Not the other way around!

6. In many cases, entrepreneurs scale up their venture to a certain extent within a few years of inception and then exit. Your thoughts on this trend?
   Sanjay: Nothing right or wrong about this. After all, it is the entrepreneur who has started the company. So he should decide when to exit. He does so when he thinks it is the right time, whatever be the reason.

7. As an investor, what kind of start-ups do you invest in? What do you look for when you evaluate start-ups for investment?
   Sanjay: I look for people and opportunities that resonate with me. If the chemistry isn't right, the arithmetic doesn't work!

8. What are the chief challenges Indian start-ups face in raising funds?
   Sanjay: The need to think big and to craft a value proposition that customers are willing to pay for. Sales

and marketing, including communication skills, are areas that are challenging for the typical Indian start-up.

9. How can I, as an entrepreneur, reach out to potential investors? What are the means available?
   Sanjay: It is a good idea to reach out to investors through a referral. Attend events that are usually frequented by investors. Become a part of various entrepreneur-focused groups. Network and ask other entrepreneurs to put you in touch with investors they may know. Use your advisors and mentors, alumni networks and social tools like LinkedIn. In fact, this is the first bar you have to set for yourself and pass! If all else fails, reach out to them through their websites, which will have a 'submit a business plan' section.

10. What should an entrepreneur look for in an investor for his/her venture? (To state it another way, how will an entrepreneur know if he/she has found the right investor?)
    Sanjay: As I said earlier, if the chemistry isn't right, the arithmetic won't work! So make sure you are comfortable with the investor with regard to their vision for the company, values, working style, understanding of your business, experience, networks and track record. Do your own research by speaking to the entrepreneurs of companies the investor has previously invested in (this list of companies is usually

available on the investor's website) and by asking around in various entrepreneur groups.

11. When looking for investors for my venture, what should I be prepared for? What kind of scenarios and questions can I expect during this process?
   Sanjay: Your passion, market, customer and business understanding must show. There are essentially five questions every investor wants answers to: i) Who are you? That is, talk about your team, their experience, capability and track record; ii) What's the problem or opportunity you are addressing? ; iii) How large is this problem/opportunity and how fast is it growing?; iv) How will you solve/address this in an innovative/unique way?; v) How will you make money?

12. Before setting up a venture, is it essential to make a business plan and projections? Why/why not?
    Sanjay: A business plan is a good idea because it helps marshal your thoughts and forces you to focus and lay out clear measureable milestones.

Funding – An Entrepreneur's Perspective

A chat with Anish Basu Roy, co-founder of Channelyst. It is an online platform for finding the right distribution partners – retailers, stockists, distributors, etc. (Check out http://www.channelyst.in/)

1. When did you set up your company? What are the services this company offers?
   Anish: Channelyst was incorporated in May 2013. We are the world's first online platform to disrupt the traditional distribution channels through aggregation of distributors, retailers and companies. We aim to enable distributors and retailers across emerging economies to manage their businesses online, thereby improving their profitability and processes.

2. What was your revenue for the financial year 2014-2015?
   Anish: We closed the financial year with a transaction value of over Rs 20 Crore. We have aggressive plans for this financial year, with projected transaction values of over Rs 1000 Crore.

3. Briefly, can you describe your company in terms of size and scale of operations – number of people, number of customers, the names of some customers, which markets you serve, etc.?
   Anish: Currently, Channelyst has over 50,000 distributors on its network and over 135 companies are using our online platform. We have a presence in over 100 districts and 45,000 localities in India. We manage our operations with a fairly lean team of under fifty employees. Most major FMCG and telecom companies use our services in India. However, what gives us tremendous satisfaction is that we have

helped nearly seventy-five small and medium-sized manufacturers expand their operations.

4. Let us talk about the time you raised funds for your company from an investor. Tell us about the circumstances at that point of time and why you decided to seek funds from outside. Also, what was the amount raised and from whom?
   Anish: Sometime around the end of 2013, we had successfully completed our 'minimum viable product' stage. We were seeing promising results and traction from our initial set of customers. This was a much-needed shot in the arm since what we were attempting to build as a business model had never been done before. It did not have a global precedent.

   We always knew right from the start that we were best positioned to solve this emerging economies-specific problem and once we had the initial traction, we would need to scale aggressively. Scale was always going to be our biggest competitive advantage.

   And so we began our fundraising journey to scale up quickly. Around this time, we were selected by TiE as one of the top ten early stage start-ups under their programme called Anthah Prerana. This gave us the required exposure to the circuit of investors at the right time.

   Around May 2014, we raised our first round of external investment from Bitchemy Ventures.

5. Why did you choose this particular source of funds? What kind of research did you do before finalizing this option?
   Anish: Anter (my co-founder) and I had a cumulative experience of nearly fifteen years behind us with companies like Nokia, Coca-Cola and P&G. Given our professional background, we were always clear about the fact that we wanted to raise funds from a professionally managed company.

   While we were soliciting investor interest, we would look at elements such as the current portfolio of the fund, its typical sweet spot and its industry/sector focus.

   Right from the time we started interacting with the Bitchemy team, we got a strong sense of mutual cultural alignment. Also, their understanding and appreciation of the space we were in was critical in sealing the partnership.

6. Until then, what had been your approach to generating funds for the business?
   Anish: Until then, like most others, we were a bootstrapped company. We recruited an ultra-lean-but-mean team of three people. Customer revenues were steady but meagre. So essentially it was mostly about dipping into all the savings we had!

7. How did you use the funds you raised from the investor? Please give us an idea of what proportion of the money went into what aspect of your venture.

Anish: We have continued to run a very tight ship even after raising the funds. Technology and on-ground execution have been our major areas of investment. Close to 35 per cent of the funds were invested in building the online platform (which our customers use) and in internal tools which improve the productivity of the on-ground team. A similar amount has been invested in building a low-cost yet hyper-productive team on the ground.

8. For entrepreneurs who want to raise funds, could you explain the process in terms of steps? What would be step one, step two, and so on?

    Anish: To my mind there are three significant stages when raising your first round of external investment for most start-ups.

    i) Internal Business Planning: It is critical to have a structured and detailed business plan which will help you decide whether you need to raise money at all, what you need to raise it for, how much exactly you need to raise and when you need to raise it.

    ii) Research and Investor Outreach: Once you have the answers to the questions above, the process of researching and reaching out to potential investors starts. Look for investors who are interested in the kind of space you are in and have a business that fits with your plans. At this stage, it makes a lot of sense to participate in external forums, contests and events because they give you a lot of visibility.

iii) Presentations, Term Sheets and Valuations: Once you have been able to secure the initial interest of a few investors, you'd mostly be living and sleeping with Excel sheets and PowerPoint documents. It is important to prepare well for this stage since most entrepreneurs don't necessarily understand the lingo of complicated term sheets and the intricacies of discounted cash flows.

9. Who helped you in your fund raising efforts? In what way did they help?
Anish: I believe it's important to have the right kind of expertise by your side while raising funds. You need it in the areas where you may not have the necessary skill.

Fortunately for us, we had batchmates with tremendous investment banking experience all over the world and an awesome accounting firm which had worked with start-ups before. I'd like to mention my investment banker schoolmate Anurag Pandey here, along with Elagaan, our accounting firm.

10. What were the key factors that helped you raise funds? In other words, what convinced the investor/lender to give you the money?
Anish: Some of the key factors which worked in our favour while raising funds were:
   i) A kick-ass team.
   ii) A tremendously detailed business plan.

iii) The fact that we were solving a unique problem and a problem specific to emerging economies which hadn't been done anywhere before.
iv) A genuine intent to create value for the entire ecosystem and impact businesses and lives.

11. In evaluating a potential investor, what are the things an entrepreneur should look out for? What will tell him/her that a particular person is the right investor for his/her venture?

    Anish: I think foremost on that list has to be what kind of involvement versus interference the investor wants to have in your business. I believe every entrepreneur will always welcome constructive involvement of the investor in the business, but unwarranted interference can be distracting.

    Secondly, figure out what kind of investment horizon the investor is looking at. An investor with an unduly short investment horizon can put inordinate pressure on a business.

    Lastly, find out what kind of people you'd be working with from the investor's side. There needs to be a strong cultural alignment with the investor team.

12. What traps do entrepreneurs usually fall into in this effort to raise funds? Any tips on how they can avoid these?

    Anish: By far, one of the largest misconceptions in entrepreneurial circuits is the importance given to fund raising itself. I mean, everybody seems to be measuring the entrepreneur based on whether he/she has raised funds or not!

Raising investment is not necessarily the only measure of success for a business; it is just one of them. The aim should be to build a profitable, impactful and sustainable business, not just a fundable one. Hence entrepreneurs need to first evaluate the need for raising funds before trying to do so.

The other thing that I often hear from entrepreneurs when investors refuse to finance their business is that the investor didn't understand the idea at all. Somewhere there is a sense of the blame being deflected towards the investor. That isn't right!

From my experience, investors who refuse to partner with you are the richest source of ideas and feedback. A refusal makes you think! It just makes you better. Some of the best iterations we've done to our business model have happened after being turned down by an investor. They have made us stronger.

The Business Plan

From my experience, I have found that a business plan is a vital document for an entrepreneur, more so in the founding stage of the venture. Like a compass, a business plan is your guide; it gives you direction and a frame of reference. Putting some thought into a business plan helps you flesh out your idea and really take an objective look at it.

While there are hundreds of versions of the business plan floating around, here are the most important aspects that a good plan will address:

- Definition of the problem/opportunity you have spotted in the market.
- The nature of the solution you are offering: How is your offering going to solve this problem/address this opportunity? Is your solution superior to or different from the solutions that may already be existing in the market? If yes, in what way?
- How will you address the problem? The method and the process flow.
- Size of the market you are aiming to address.
- Competitive landscape: Who will be your main competitors; strength, weakness, opportunity and threat (SWOT) analysis of each main competitor.
- Composition of your team: experience and skills of each member of the founding team; what makes your team relevant and attractive for the business you are entering; the strengths that each member brings to the venture.
- Risks and their mitigation: What are the risks you anticipate in setting up this venture; what precautions are you taking in order to avoid/minimize the resultant damage to your venture?
- Revenue model: How will your venture earn money?
- Brand strategy: the definition of the targeted consumer segment. What will be the unique value proposition of your brand to this consumer? What compelling reason

are you giving the consumer to buy your offering? What are the core values of your brand?
- Marketing plan: How will you generate visibility and 'pull' for your business from your targeted consumer segment?
- Business development plan and process: the step-by-step process by which you will reach prospective customers, pitch your offers to them, convince them and bag their orders.
- Targeted financials: the turnover (revenue) and profit/loss your venture is realistically likely to achieve in each of the first three years after inception.
- Funds: Do you need external funds? If yes, when and how much? How will you use those funds?

For more details, speak to your mentor or a few seasoned entrepreneurs.

Resources

Here is a list of some organizations and incubators along with some other useful information when you think of becoming an entrepreneur. Please note that this is not a comprehensive list.

Organizations

- *National Entrepreneurship Network (NEN)*: www.nenonline.org. Over the last ten years, NEN has helped create the student entrepreneur ecosystem in India. It continues to do some superlative work in this field.
  You should also check out NEN's blog at www.nenonline.org/blog-home
- *The Indus Entrepreneurs (TiE)*: www.tie.org
- *Indian Angel Network*: www.indianangelnetwork.com

Incubators and Accelerators

- *TLabs*: www.tlabs.in
- *Microsoft Ventures*: www.microsoftventures.com/accelerators/

- *Startup Village*: www.startupvillage.in
- *The Startup Centre*: www.thestartupcentre.com
- *Villgro*: www.villgro.org
- The Department of Science and Technology of the Government of India has set up Technology Business Incubators (TBIs) across India. To get a list of TBIs visit: www.nstedb.com/institutional/tbi-center.htm
- First100Sales: www.first100sales.com
- Growth Enabler: growthenabler.com/growth

Programmes, Platforms and Media Resources

- *Tata First Dot*, powered by NEN: A platform that picks the most promising student start-ups every year. www.tatafirstdot.com
- *The Pitch*, a business reality show on Bloomberg TV. www.facebook.com/yourpitch
- *Power of Ideas (POI)*: An annual competition organized by the *Economic Times* in association with the Centre for Innovation, Incubation and Entrepreneurship, (CIIE) IIM Ahmedabad and the Department of Science and Technology (DST), Government of India. – www.facebook.com/EconomicTimes ThePowerofIdeas
- Mukund Mohan's blog which I find very informative and insightful: www.bestengagingcommunities.com/
- *Your Story*, a news portal for entrepreneurs: www.yourstory.com

Gracias

Sunita Singh, Sri Krishna, Sujaya Rao and Mischelle of NEN. For putting me in touch with student entrepreneurs and supplying me with some statistics. And for supporting this effort wholeheartedly.

Sanjay Anandaram – investor, mentor to start-ups, entrepreneurship evangelist. For readily answering my questions on enterprise funding (read the chapter 'Funding Fundas') and for other invaluable inputs.

Mr Ravikumar and Professor Ranganathan. For your kind words of encouragement and support.

My family and all my friends, especially Anand Narayan, Sonali, Madalasa, Ramkumar and Prasad. For constantly egging me on from the sidelines.

Manoj Kunisseri and Tuhin Ghosh. For reading the drafts of the stories in this book and offering valuable suggestions to make the book better.

Sheetal Iyer, Kaustubh Dhargalkar and Sijo George. For putting me in touch with student entrepreneurs.

All the entrepreneurs featured in this book. But for you, this book would never have been!

Karthika, Debasri, Rea and Bonita at HarperCollins India.

Charu, my alter ego. For staying up with me till late in the night, several nights in a row. For being the first to read every page of this book and critique it objectively. And for gamely putting up with my tortoise-like tendency to withdraw into a shell for long spells, emerging only once in a while.

Without exception, all of you made me believe that this was a project worth undertaking, a story worth telling. I can't thank you enough!

And finally, Chikkoo. For making me see life through the eyes of a four-year-old. And for providing me with regular doses of madness and laughter.

If I have inadvertently missed someone out, I have only my premature dotage to blame. You know who you are and what you have done for this book. Thank you very much!